The Miracle of Tongues

The Miracle of Tongues

By
Don Basham

Fleming H. Revell Company

Old Tappan, New Jersey

ISBN 0-8007-0632-3

Library of Congress Catalog Card Number: 73-21974

Contents

Introduction

The interdenominational meeting in a large city auditorium was drawing to a close. The speaker had concluded his message on the work of the Holy Spirit and had invited questions. A distinguished looking man in his fifties quickly stood up.

"What is your question, sir?" the speaker asked.

"May I come to the platform?" The man moved forward without waiting for an answer. Reaching the speaker's side, he took the microphone and turned to the congregation with a stern expression.

"I'm an attorney and a member of the First Christian Church in this city," he began. "I've been a Christian for over thirty years, an elder in my church for sixteen years, and chairman of the administrative board for the last five years.

"I came tonight at the invitation of a couple in our church to learn something about this new religious 'thing' they've gotten involved with."

He glanced at the speaker and his stern expression tightened into a scowl. "I don't know what I expected," he went on, "but I certainly cannot accept what I heard. I am shocked at the blatant form of mysticism this man advocates. I do not believe it is Christian and I say people involved in such mysticism have no place in our churches. As for me, I want no part of what I heard tonight!"

Then, practically throwing the microphone back to the speaker, he strode angrily out of the auditorium.

The incident just described is admittedly dramatic. Nevertheless, it is a true reflection of a genuine spiritual tension in the church today. Fresh winds of spiritual renewal are sweeping through the musty corridors of institutional Christianity, raising frequent and disturbing clouds of dust. The common expression used to identify this fresh breeze is "Charismatic renewal," with the word *charismatic* referring to the miraculous gifts and ministries of the Holy Spirit described in the New Testament which are re-emerging in the life of the church today.

Yet, as the above incident reflects, this renewal is not without its problems and its critics. As one who for the last six years has been regularly engaged in a writing and teaching ministry interpreting this move to the church, I have been present more than once when such controversy and criticism flared into the open.

In fact, I was the speaker on the occasion just described.

But we should be neither surprised nor perturbed when such controversy appears. Every revival in the history of Christianity has had its share of critics and detractors. Actually, they serve a valid and necessary function, since every revival has also had its share of zealots and heretics. Excesses have resulted in splinter groups which seem determined to major in emotional extremes, strange practices, and corresponding exclusivism. Such extremes need criticism and correction, but even without a heretical fringe the charismatic renewal has problems. Why? Because renewal brings power, and power always brings problems.

Renewal inevitably challenges the established ecclesiastical order; it clashes with orthodox complacency. Jesus himself said,

> Neither do men put new wine into old bottles, else the bottles break, and the wine runneth out and the bottles perish; but they put new wine into new bottles, and both are preserved.
>
> Matthew 9:17

Central to the charismatic renewal in Christianity we find the experience called the gift of or baptism in the Holy Spirit. While the New Testament speaks of this Holy Spirit baptism as a separate experience of empowering which follows conversion, many Christians fail to see the distinction. Conversion or being "born again," is the encounter with Jesus Christ as Saviour, which makes one a Christian. The Baptism in the Holy Spirit is a second encounter with Jesus Christ, this time as Baptizer in the Holy Spirit, which endues the Christian with power for service. The need for this empowering is clearly described in Scripture.

When Jesus commissioned his disciples to go and preach (Matthew 28:18–20), he also commanded them not to go until they received the spiritual power necessary to fulfill the commission.

> And being assembled together with them, [He] commanded them that they should not depart from Jerusalem, but wait for the promise of the Father, which, saith he, ye have heard of me. For John truly baptized with water; but ye shall be baptized with the Holy Ghost not many days hence . . . But ye shall receive power, after that the Holy Ghost is come upon you; and ye shall be witnesses unto me both in Jerusalem, and in all Judea, and in Samaria, and unto the uttermost parts of the earth.
>
> Acts 1:4–5,8

Failure to recognize the reality of both these experiences is cause for some of the current confusion about the charismatic movement.

But still more of the confusion is caused by the phenomenon of speaking in tongues which accompanies the Baptism in the Holy Spirit. If the phrase, Baptism in the Holy Spirit, causes temperatures to rise, speaking in tongues causes them to boil over! As John Sherrill, in his classic book *They Speak With Other Tongues,* succinctly put it, "Tongues make people fight."

To pinpoint the beginning of the controversy over speaking in tongues we must go all the way back to the Day of Pentecost, for from the moment tongues first appeared, those who heard them were divided in their opinions. Some who heard agreed it was a miracle.

> And they were all amazed and marvelled, saying one to another, Behold, are not all these which speak Galileans? And how hear we every man in our own tongue, wherein we were born? . . . we do hear them speak in our tongues the wonderful works of God.
> Acts 2:7–8,11

Others, obviously unable to identify the languages spoken, accused the disciples of being drunk.

> Others mocking, said, These men are full of new wine.
> Acts 2:13

As the author of several books attempting to interpret the present-day reality of the charismatic gifts of the Holy Spirit in the church, I frequently receive letters reflecting the attitudes, both positive and negative, which speaking in tongues fosters among Christians. Here are two typical examples.

April 30, 1972
Dear Reverend Basham,

I'm writing to thank you for the help I received from reading your book *Face Up With a Miracle.* It helped greatly to open my understanding to the wonderful things God is doing in the church today. I had heard about miracles happening by the power of God, but in all my years as a member of the church, I had never seen anything happen to anybody which convinced me that God still did miraculous, exciting things for people. But I knew that if such things *were* true, and God *could* bless people in miraculous ways like He did in Bible times, I wanted in on it.

At first your book was only interesting, but as I got deeper into it, I began to think that if this business about the Baptism in the Holy Spirit and speaking in tongues was real, maybe I could have it. I started to pray for it long before I finished your book, and by the time I finished I had received, and was praising God in tongues. What a truly wonderful way to pray! And the Lord has become so preciously real to me now! But that's not all.

The day after I received the Baptism and spoke in tongues my wife started seeking, too. She locked the doors, put the children to bed for a nap, and got down on her knees and received the Baptism with the gift of singing in tongues. Praise the Lord!

And that was just the beginning of a series of blessings that has my head spinning and my heart praising God. Two weeks later my minister and his wife received the Baptism with tongues. Next, my younger brother received Jesus as His Saviour. Then my father, who is sixty years old, accepted Jesus as his Saviour, and he and my mother joined our church. Two weeks later my father received the Baptism with a beautiful prayer language. A few days later my younger sister also received the Baptism with tongues. The latest to be blessed is my secretary at work. She also has received.

I never knew the Christian life could be so exciting and am praying that the revival that has blessed our family and our church will sweep the whole world.

May God bless you,
G.M.
Seattle, Washington

But along with the letters of gratitude and praise for what God is doing, come some letters of criticism and rejection. Here's one:

October 11, 1972
Dear Mr. Basham,

I have just finished reading your book *Face Up With a Miracle*. It is a very clever book, but what you write about tongue speaking is deceiving and dangerous. I have been around people who claim to speak in tongues since I was a small child, and foreign languages have not been spoken miraculously, as on the Day of Pentecost, since the end of the first century. What do you expect to gain by deceiving people?

I take it that the alleged "tongues" has really added nothing worthwhile to your life or anyone else's. Your belief in speaking in tongues (if you really do believe in them) is a product of your own imagination. I have heard it too many times to be fooled. What people call "tongues" is certainly not a foreign language; it's only hysterical babbling. How can a trained minister, a seminary graduate at that, pretend to believe such foolishness? Perhaps you are sincere, but if so, you are sincerely in error.

As an educated clergyman, surely you must realize that before Christianity, pagans spoke in so-called tongues. Why, then, call the experience Christian? Or why be so picky in performing or exercising apostolic gifts? Why just speaking in tongues and no poison drinking or snake handling?

Besides, in the New Testament, speaking in tongues was used to win unbelievers. But today it is used only to let a Christian brag about how big and important he is before other Christians.

Speaking in tongues has always split the church into *have* and *have-nots,* into superior and inferior. Not all Christians in the New Testament spoke in tongues, but they were not inferior to you or to any other Christian who makes the claim to tongues.

Indeed, I haven't seen that tongues (so-called) have ever helped anyone's relationship to Christ or to his fellow men, but I have seen such claims do a lot of damage and hinder a lot of Christians. In fact, the most immoral Christians I know claim the gift of tongues, and the more I learn about those who use tongues the more fearful I am of them. I'm fearful of their possible influence even on me, and I've been a Christian for a long long time.

Psychologists and psychiatrists all agree that your so-called speaking in tongues will lead to mental breakdown and even schizophrenia.

You know as well as I that speaking in tongues, and other such "miracles," is not necessary to being a Christian. All of us can be the best Christians possible under all circumstances without such trappings. Your claims are superfluous and a real hindrance, if not a real danger, to Christianity. I do not expect you to reply to this letter.

Sincerely yours,
C.R.T.
Richmond, Virginia

These letters simply confirm that the controversy over speaking in tongues, which began minutes after it first appeared on the Day of Pentecost, still rages today. Those who experience the Baptism in the Holy Spirit with the evidence of speaking in tongues know the experience and the tongues are real, and they rejoice; while others, not seeing and not understanding, criticize or condemn the practice outright. And that very controversy provides the basis for this book.

Don W. Basham

Chapter 1

What They Say About Speaking in Tongues

In this first chapter, we will consider the point of view which questions or rejects altogether the experience of speaking in tongues. In order to present the opposing point of view, we will be quoting three nationally known Christian leaders: the late Dr. E. Stanley Jones, well-known missionary and spiritual leader of Methodism; Dr. W. A. Criswell, pastor of the First Baptist Church of Dallas, Texas, and past president of the Southern Baptist Convention; and Dr. Richard DeHaan, teacher of the popular Radio Bible Class of Grand Rapids, Michigan.

Each of these men is known to be a committed Christian and a highly effective communicator of the gospel. That we challenge their positions on the Baptism in the Holy Spirit and speaking in tongues should in no way be construed as a criticism of their total ministries. Each is author of widely-distributed statements, questioning or rejecting the validity of all modern accounts of speaking in tongues. Dr. E. Stanley Jones's point of view is expressed in a pamphlet entitled *The Holy Spirit and The Gift of Tongues;* Dr. Richard DeHaan's teaching on the subject is found in a booklet entitled *Speaking in Tongues;* while Dr. Criswell expresses his views in chapter 14 of his book *The Baptism, Filling and Gifts of the Holy Spirit.*

The theological positions of the three men indicate they have differing views concerning the reality of the Baptism in the Holy Spirit for Christians today. Stanley Jones recognizes the need for a separate empowering experience beyond conversion while both DeHaan and Criswell assume the Holy Spirit is fully received at conversion. In addition, Jones admits that speaking in tongues *may,* on occasion, accompany the infilling of the Holy Spirit, while DeHaan, a dispensationalist, asserts tongues are not possible today, and Criswell views their reappearance as "a tragedy."

The major points of criticism of speaking in tongues which are common to all three men are:

1. Speaking in tongues is not the evidence of Baptism in the Holy Spirit.
2. Not every Christian should speak in tongues.
3. Speaking in tongues is always hurtful and divisive to the Body of Christ.
4. Speaking in tongues is always induced, it never happens spontaneously.
5. Speaking in tongues is never in a known language as on the day of Pentecost.

Now we will list each of the five criticisms separately, giving brief quotes from each of the three ministers, followed by comments of our own.

1. Speaking in tongues is not the evidence of Baptism in the Holy Spirit.

E. Stanley Jones: "Can we doubt that some people today are filled with the Holy Spirit and speak in tongues as a part of the experience? I believe this happens. But not necessarily. Millions have been filled with the Holy Spirit and never speak in tongues."

Richard DeHaan: "The book of Acts certainly does not support the contention of those who say that the gift of tongues is a sign that one has received the Holy Spirit."

W.A. Criswell: "The basic doctrine that lies back of glossolalian practice is wrong. That doctrine is this: that speaking in tongues is the necessary evidence of the filling (they use the word *'Baptism')* of the Holy Spirit. This doctrine is in direct opposition to the distinct and emphasized teaching of the word of God."

Now let us take a look at the Scriptures themselves. The Book of Acts records five separate incidents where the Holy Spirit was poured out in what is called the Pentecostal experience. Here are the five Scriptures and a brief description of what took place in each incident.

Acts 2:1—21

The Day of Pentecost — On this initial occasion — sometimes referred to as the birthday of the church — the Holy Spirit was poured out on the one hundred and twenty disciples in the Upper Room. This took place in fulfillment of Jesus' promise to them that they would receive power "after the Holy Ghost came upon them" (Acts 1:8). In fact, Jesus had warned his disciples to remain in Jerusalem until they received the empowering He desired them to have. Thus, the primary purpose of receiving the gift of, or Baptism in, the Holy Spirit was to be endued with power to minister.

But at the very moment the disciples were filled with the Holy Spirit, the supernatural experience of speaking in tongues was manifested, even as Jesus had predicted it would in Mark 16:17. (This account in Acts, chapter 2, also records "the sound of a rushing mighty wind," and "cloven tongues as of fire," just *before* the Holy Spirit fell on the disciples, phenomena which are not repeated in later outpourings). The single miraculous manifestation which coincided with the receiving of the Holy Spirit was "speaking in tongues."

> And they were all filled with the Holy Ghost, and began to speak in other tongues as the Spirit gave them utterance.
>
> Acts 2:4

So with the dramatic *inward* spiritual empowering of the Holy Spirit, there came the dramatic *outward* manifestation of speaking in tongues.

Acts 8:4–17

The Outpouring in Samaria — In this second account of the outpouring of the Holy Spirit, Philip, one of the first deacons ordained in the church, began to preach the gospel in a certain Samaritan city. Signs and wonders accompanied his message and many accepted Christ, were healed, delivered from the torment of evil spirits, and baptized in water and joined to the body of Christ.

Yet none of these new converts received the Baptism in the Holy Spirit until Peter and John came down from Jerusalem to pray for them. While there is no specific mention of speaking in tongues or any other miraculous phenomenon accompanying the receiving of the Holy Spirit by the Samaritans, nevertheless *something visible or audible* must have taken place, for when Simon the magician saw whatever it was, he offered money to Peter and John in an effort to buy the ability to transmit the Holy Spirit (Acts 8:18).

Now what did Simon the magician "see"? Many leading Bible scholars agree that Simon must have seen the Samaritan Christians speaking in tongues. For example, Adam Clarke in his well-known commentary flatly states that Simon was impressed "by hearing them speak with tongues and work miracles."

So we see that in this second Pentecostal experience, although speaking in tongues is not listed per se, it is clearly implied.

Acts 8:1–19

Paul's "Pentecost" — The third account we find is in Acts, chapter 9, in which Paul meets Jesus on the road to Damascus in the Scripture's most dramatic conversion. However, he does not receive the infilling of the Holy Spirit in that conversion experience. Blinded by the encounter, Paul is led into Damascus, where he fasts and prays for three days, until an obscure disciple named Ananias is directed by God to come and pray for him to receive both his sight and the Baptism in the Holy Spirit (Acts 9:17).

While reference to speaking in tongues is omitted from the text here, we know that either at that time or subsequently Paul received tongues, for he boasted of the experience in his first letter to Corinth.

I thank my God I speak in tongues more than you all . . . .
I Corinthians 14:18

If Paul did not receive tongues at the time he was filled with the Holy Spirit, when did he? It is reasonable to assume that in his case, as on the Day of Pentecost, the tongues came at the time he received the Holy Spirit.

Acts 10:1–46

Pentecost at the House of Cornelius — In this fourth

account, we find Peter preaching the gospel to the household of Cornelius. At the point in his sermon where he proclaims forgiveness of sins for all who believe in Jesus, the Gentile listeners do not need to hear the good news twice. They accept Christ, and immediately afterward — even while Peter is still preaching — they are filled with the Holy Spirit and begin to speak in tongues.

Here tongues appeared with the infilling of the Holy Spirit, much as they did at the first Pentecost. And even though on this occasion the languages are not identified, Peter, when he reports on the experience back in Jerusalem, equates the two experiences.

> Forasmuch then as God gave them the like gift as he did unto us, who believed on the Lord Jesus Christ; what was I, that I could withstand God?
>
> Acts 11:17

Acts 19:1—6

The Ephesian Pentecost — The fifth and final report of the Pentecostal experience in Scripture is found in Acts, chapter 19, where Paul ministers to twelve Ephesian disciples. Seemingly aware that their Christian experience did not measure up to that of other believers, Paul asks, "Have ye received the Holy Ghost since ye believed?"

From their response Paul learns that, although they are believers in Jesus, they have experienced neither Christian baptism in water nor the gift of the Holy Spirit. After baptizing the twelve in water, he lays on hands and prays for them, and they all receive the Holy Spirit and begin to speak in tongues and to prophesy.

To recap, then: of the five scriptural accounts of the

Pentecostal experience, speaking in tongues is the stated evidence in three, and is clearly implied in the other two. On the basis of this, what are we to conclude? That in the New Testament church, while there may have been exceptions, speaking in tongues appears to have been the *normative* experience accompanying the Baptism in the Holy Spirit.

2. **Not every Christian should speak in tongues.**

E. Stanley Jones: "Paul asks, 'Do all possess gifts of healing? Do all speak with tongues? Do all interpret?' (I Corinthians 12:30) Meaning they do not. And yet they have the gift of the Holy Spirit."

Richard DeHaan: "He (Paul) makes it very clear to these Corinthian Christians that God did not intend for all to speak in tongues. The seven questions he asks in I Corinthians 12:29–30 clearly demand a negative answer."

W. A. Criswell: "Paul says that all the Christians at Corinth had been baptized by the Holy Spirit, had been added to the body of Christ. But in I Corinthians 12:28–30 Paul avows that all do not speak with tongues."

All three men cite Paul's question, "Do all speak with tongues?" as scriptural proof that not all Christians are supposed to speak in tongues. Yet all three men ignore Paul's later statement, "I would that ye *all* spake with tongues . . . ." (I Corinthians 14:5). Would Paul be so inconsistent as to say in one breath, "I don't expect all of you to speak in tongues," then in the next breath contradict himself and say, "I want all of you to speak in tongues"? Hardly.

Then how do we account for the seeming inconsistency? The answer is fairly simple. Critics of speaking in tongues frequently overlook the different ways the gift appears in the New Testament. First, there is the use of tongues in prayer and praise for the spiritual edification of the worshiper. This was the use for tongues when they appeared in the Book of Acts in chapters two, ten, and nineteen. Here are some scriptural statements referring to the devotional use of tongues.

1. ". . . we do hear them speak in our tongues the wonderful works of God" (Acts 2:11).

2. "For they heard them speak with tongues and magnify God" (Acts 10:46).

3. "And when Paul had laid his hands upon them, the Holy Ghost came on them; and they spake with tongues, and prophesied" (Acts 19:6).

4. "For he that speaketh in an unknown tongue speaketh not unto men, but unto God . . . in the spirit he speaketh mysteries" (I Corinthians 14:2).

5. "He that speaketh in an unknown tongue edifieth himself . . ." (I Corinthians 14:4).

6. "I would that ye all spake with tongues . . ." (I Corinthians 14:5).

7. "For if I pray in an unknown tongue, my spirit prayeth, but my understanding is unfruitful" (I Corinthians 14:14).

8. "I thank my God, I speak with tongues more than ye all . . ." (I Corinthians 14:18).

We should also note that there are no restrictions on using tongues in this way — no limit concerning how much, how many or how often. For example, on the day of Pentecost *all* the one hundred and twenty disciples spoke in tongues. In Acts 10, the Holy Spirit fell on *all* Cornelius' household and *all* began to speak in tongues. In Ephesus, Paul prayed for twelve disciples to receive the Holy Spirit and *all twelve* began to speak in tongues.

But Paul also explains there is a second use for tongues. Tongues are also to be used in the public services of worship, but on a highly restricted basis. A message in tongues in the assembly was to be followed by the gift of interpretation of tongues, that the assembled congregation could understand what was taking place. Here are some Scriptures referring to this use of tongues.

1. " . . . for greater is he that prophesieth than he that speaketh with tongues, except he interpret, that the church may receive edifying" (I Corinthians 14:5).
2. "Wherefore let him that speaketh in an unknown tongue pray that he may interpret" (I Corinthians 14:13).
3. "If any man speak in an unknown tongue, let it be by two, or at the most three, and that by course; and let one interpret." (I Corinthians 14:27).
4. "Do all speak with tongues?" (I Corinthians 12:30)

From these passages it is clear that when tongues appear in the public worship service, they should be interpreted so that the whole congregation can benefit from the manifestation of the gifts. And if there is no interpreter, the one speaking in tongues can still use the gift, provided he does it quietly, beneath his breath so as not to disturb the other worshipers. " . . . let him keep silence in the church and speak to himself and God" (I Corinthians 14:28).

Gift or Ministry?

Still another point needs to be made concerning Paul's statement, "Do all speak with tongues?" Seen in context, this Scripture does not refer to one of the *gifts* of the Holy Spirit which Paul lists in the beginning of chapter twelve. Here Paul is speaking of *ministries* God has set in the church. By "ministry," I believe Paul means one's major contribution to the body of Christ. It represents his "job" in the church. And, as Paul points out, not everyone has the same job. Just as some Christians may be called to the ministry of an apostle or a prophet, so others may be called to the ministry of speaking in tongues. So, taking into account Paul's statements about both gifts and ministries, let's notice these facts: (1) Paul wants everyone to speak in tongues for his own spiritual development and personal edification (I Corinthians 14:4–5); (2) But not every person who speaks in tongues for his own spiritual benefit will have a *ministry* of bringing messages in tongues publicly for interpretation.

So, if we may paraphrase Paul's words: "I thank God I speak in tongues more than all of you, and I want all of you to speak in tongues also, because it is spiritually edifying for you. But not everyone of you who speaks in tongues privately will be called to a public ministry of speaking in the kind of tongues which must be interpreted. Some of you will have such a ministry, but not all."

The distinction between gifts and ministries is further illustrated when Paul describes the *gift* of prophecy and the *ministry* of a prophet. Concerning the *gift* of prophecy he says,

> For ye may all prophesy one by one, that all may learn and all may be comforted.
>
> I Corinthians 14:31

No statement could be more clear. Every Spirit-baptized Christian has access to the gift of prophecy. But concerning the *ministry* of a prophet Paul says, "Are all prophets?" (I Corinthians 12:29) By which he means no, not all are prophets. Again let us paraphrase: "Everyone of you may exercise the gift of prophecy so that all of you may learn and be comforted by that spiritual gift. But not all of you who use the *gift* of prophecy are called to the *ministry* of a prophet. Some of you will be, but not all."

As with prophecy, so with tongues. When Paul says, "I would that ye all spake with tongues . . ." he's speaking of the use of tongues for personal spiritual edification. When he says, "Do all speak with tongues?" he refers to the ministry of speaking in tongues for interpretation which some will be given, but not all.

We trust the distinctions we have outlined will serve to correct both misunderstanding and misapplication of Paul's statement, "Do all speak with tongues?"

3. Speaking in tongues is always divisive and hurtful.

E. Stanley Jones: "To bind up the possession of the Holy Spirit with the possession of the gift of tongues is, to my mind, perhaps the greatest spiritual disaster that has struck this confused and groping age . . . . No wonder then, the use of tongues has always been divisive."

Richard DeHaan: "We must insist, however, in love, that the exercise of so-called tongues speaking has brought much confusion and harm to the church. Congregations have been torn apart through problems arising out of it. Not only does this practice cause division and spiritual frustration, it also has led some to gross carnality."

W.A. Criswell: "Wherever and whenever glossolalia appears, it is always hurtful and divisive. There is no exception to this. It is but another instrument for the tragic torture of the body of Christ. I have seen some of our finest churches torn apart by the practice."

The criticism leveled here has some justification. Many times when the Baptism in the Holy Spirit with speaking in tongues appears in non-pentecostal churches, temperatures rise and tempers flare. Excited over their empowering experience, newly Spirit-baptized Christians often say too much too soon. More zealous than loving and more enthusiastic than wise, their ill-timed testimonies often seem to run roughshod over traditions and experiences cherished by non-charismatics. This can lead in a moment to the erection of barriers which may take months of patient teaching and loving explanation to clear away. In the interval, the ongoing work of the kingdom of God may have been more hindered than helped.

Charles and Frances Hunter, in their helpful book *The Two Sides of a Coin*, give an excellent illustration of the reaction which may result from the heavy-handed or ill-timed question or testimony. Frances says,

> Can I share with you a question that has really bugged me many times? Over and over, after I had shared in a service where the Spirit of the Lord had really been poured out and many people had found Christ, someone would come up to me with a complete lack of love and haughtily ask, "Have you received the baptism with the Holy Spirit?" I don't know anything which can turn a person away from this beautiful gift of God faster than to have someone with a super superior attitude ask them this question.

But having admitted that tongue-speaking Christians at times exhibit an appalling lack of sensitivity, two other things must also be said. First, while people may misuse God's gifts and speak of them in an unwise or unloving manner, this in no way invalidates the gifts. Secondly, the critics of tongues share equally in any pain or divisiveness by refusing to recognize something real and vital has happened in the life of the one testifying. *Resistance* to the gift of tongues is as much a part of the problem as an unwise testimony to their reality.

Experience clearly shows how any fresh manifestation of the Holy Spirit, speaking in tongues, healing, prophecy, etc., may threaten religious complacency and prompt dark mutterings of "hurtful and divisive" from defenders of the status quo. For them, the thought of genuine spiritual renewal can be most unsettling.

Years ago, a young woman in the church I pastored in Toronto, Canada, received a remarkable healing in our midweek prayer meeting. For weeks, she had appeared in church on crutches; then, one Sunday, she walked in on two strong, straight legs. But when she tried to explain to various church friends how God had healed her, she met only skepticism and rebuke. Shaken and confused by their hostility, she later confessed to me, "It's hard to understand, but most of the people I've witnessed to would be greatly relieved to see me back on crutches."

We would suggest it is not the outward sign of healing or speaking in tongues which leads to rejection so much as what these external signs point to. Tongues, we must remember, do not stand alone. They are an outward sign God is doing something new and wonderful for people. This is the personal testimony of millions of Christians today. If speaking in tongues was all that happened at Pentecost, the day would soon have been lost to history. But the appearance of tongues signified an unleashing of power which changed the disciples from a frightened group of disillusioned men into a band of bold and fearless witnesses for the Lord Jesus Christ.

So, spiritual renewal inevitably results in a mixture of blessings and problems. Those involved in the renewal thank God for it, while many of those outside the renewal criticize and condemn it.

But fortunately, many Christian leaders, who are *not* involved in the charismatic renewal with its emphasis on spiritual gifts, still recognize its validity. Recently I sat in the office of a leading Southern Baptist pastor who is *not* charismatic. When the conversation turned to speaking in tongues, he frankly commented, "I believe it because the Scriptures teach it, and I'm convinced that most problems which arise in churches where the Baptism in the Holy Spirit and speaking in tongues appear come not from those who receive the experience but rather from those who reject it. The Baptism in the Holy Spirit and speaking in tongues presents no threat to me or to my people."

4. Speaking in tongues is always induced: it never happens spontaneously.

E. Stanley Jones: "Moreover, this must be said; only where it is taught that tongues accompanies the coming of the Holy Spirit does this phenomenon occur . . . In these modern manifestations of speaking in tongues it is not only taught, it is often induced."

Richard DeHaan: "It is tragic, yet true, that a person may sincerely believe he is exercising a genuine gift from God, while in actuality he is playing a trick on himself. Psychologists tell us that it is an emotional exercise which can be induced in various manners. Many people who have come out of the Pentecostal movement are now convinced that they have been deceiving themselves."

W. A. Criswell: "Seekers after the 'baptism' are encouraged to remain in 'tarrying meetings' in which they are taught to loosen the tongue by imitation of the leader in saying 'ah-bah, ah'bah, beta, beta,' etc. The leader will shake the lower jaw of a seeker to loosen it so that the gift will come. What am I to think about all of this? Is the Holy Third Person of the Trinity . . . thus controlled and directed by the loosening of the joints of the jaw? By the gibberish of senseless sounds?"

The implication behind these criticisms is that speaking in tongues is not a genuine spiritual gift; therefore people must be psychologically or emotionally tricked into experiencing them. The truth is, many Christians have received the Baptism in the Holy Spirit with speaking in tongues while praying alone. My own son-in-law received the Baptism with speaking in tongues in such a manner.

A few years ago, in the company of Christian friends, I made a trip into Eastern Europe and for several days enjoyed precious fellowship with the persecuted Christians there. In Budapest, Hungary, we met a pastor who had been dismissed from his church. Revival had broken out and the congregation was beginning to grow. Therefore, he had been removed by the state authorities and had been replaced by a state-approved communist leader.

According to the pastor's own testimony, the revival had broken out after he received the Baptism in the Holy Spirit with speaking in tongues and began to preach with new power. *He had never heard of anyone speaking in tongues before it happened to him.* But one day as he had knelt alone in the little church praying for God to use him more effectively, he received the Holy Spirit and began to praise the Lord "in a wonderful new way."

Are people who speak in tongues psychologically duped? Emotionally deceived? The same accusation can be leveled at any minister who issues an altar call for people to accept Jesus Christ as Saviour. For years Dr. Billy Graham was criticized for inviting people in a mass meeting to make a decision for Christ.

"An appeal to sheer emotionalism!" his critics fumed. "Mass hysteria!" many liberal clergymen complained.

I can recall the evaluation of Graham's ministry made by one of my own seminary professors: "More or less harmless. Graham's preaching does little harm, but certainly no great good."

It is obvious that a person may respond to an invitation to accept Christ for invalid reasons with the result that his commitment later proves meaningless, but such occasional examples hardly invalidate the reality of the conversion of millions of other Christians.

Perhaps for similarly unsound reasons, a Christian may seek the Baptism in the Holy Spirit with speaking in tongues and end up with something less than a genuine experience. But again we would insist that such occasional examples hardly invalidate the reality of the experience of millions of other Christians whose spiritual empowering is demonstrably real.

5. Speaking in tongues today is never in a known language as on the Day of Pentecost.

E. Stanley Jones: "The gift of tongues is unintelligible utterance . . . . This differentiates it from the tongues used at Pentecost. There 'every man heard in his own language the wonderful works of God . . . .' This type of tongues has apparently not reappeared in its modern expression . . . . The Pentecost type of tongues is not available [today]."

Richard DeHaan: "We hear reports that on some occasions uneducated people today speak perfect Chinese, Hebrew, or some other difficult language but we have never seen these reports confirmed."

W. A. Criswell: "As far as I have been able to learn, no real language is ever spoken by the glossolaliast. He truly speaks in an unknown and unknowable tongue."

The claim that speaking in tongues today is never in a known language, the insistence that "Pentecost is an unrepeatable experience," brings us to the major purpose of this book. Here we are dealing with *the* basic question: Is speaking in tongues a genuine manifestation of the Spirit of God or not? Is it real or is it fake?

Essentially, all objections to speaking in tongues revolve around this crucial point. If it can be reliably demonstrated that, on occasion, the tongues are in known languages, understood by those hearing them as on the Day of Pentecost, then we are faced with the kind of miracle our three distinguished critics insist cannot happen.

Once such confirmation is established, then other — even legitimate — criticisms which may arise must be seen in an entirely different light. Abuses and misuses of tongues may exist, even as they did at Corinth, but the basic issue is settled; *tongues are real,* and God is at work in a supernatural way among His people!

The chapters which follow consist of such testimonies, most of them publicly unreported until now. We trust they will prove inspiring for the many charismatic Christians for whom the reality of tongues is no longer a question, and convincing to many other sincere but skeptical Christians as well.

Chapter 2

I Forgave the Lord
for My Embarrassment

May 30, 1972
Dear Don,

Blessings in the name of our Lord.

Some weeks ago I received a magazine clipping about your request for tongues in a known language and would have written sooner but have been busy with prescheduled speaking engagements. In line with your request, there have been several times when the Holy Spirit has spoken through me in another language, either in prayer or praise, and someone present has been familiar with the language.

Over forty years ago I was filled with Spirit, but was unwilling to be used by Him for quite some time. In the late 1940's I was present at a dedication of a new church here in Fort Worth. Many out-of-town visitors were present, as well as various religious dignitaries. After a great struggle with myself, I finally yielded to the Spirit and a message came in another tongue. A kind of holy pause followed, but there was no interpretation. I felt crucified! In the first place, I had not wanted to be used of God in the presence of so many ministers.

In the service that night, however, a Greek friend of mine came to me and said, "You speak Greek!" He had brought his business partner to the dedication service that afternoon, a man who was also a Greek, and what the Spirit had said through me had brought real fear to the man. The words spoken were, "God the Father is in this place; God the Son is in this place; and God the Holy Spirit is in this place."

My friend, Mr. Chokas, had experienced difficulty in restraining his partner from coming to me to enjoy a conversation in Greek. He kept saying, "But she speaks Greek!" On hearing how the Holy Spirit had worked, I was comforted and forgave the Lord for my fear and embarrassment.

Another time I was praying with two friends, a Baptist and a Disciple of Christ. Although I felt close to both of them, I had never spoken in tongues in their presence. This time we were praying over an urgent matter and I felt constrained to pray in the Spirit. Afterwards, I was conversing with the Lord in English. My friend from the Disciples of Christ church was weeping and said to me, "Thelma, I know you do not know verbs and tenses in the Spanish language, yet you prayed in perfect Spanish, and the strange thing is that after you prayed in Spanish, you prayed exactly the same words in English."

One other beautiful incident happened some years ago. I was praying with a few friends and after my prayer burden lifted, I was caught up in worship and was quietly singing a song of worship to the Lord. When I opened my eyes, kneeling there beside me with her face bathed in tears was an Hungarian woman. Her name was Elena. Elena is Hungarian nobility and highly educated. She began to say to me, "Thelma, you were singing in a most beautiful tongue, a language that is dead today. It is not Latin, it is not Italian, it is the high Roman language that is little known; and you were singing words of worship, glorifying God in His majesty and power and love."

It is a blessed privilege to share these experiences with you, Don. May God continue to bless you in your work for Him.

Your friend,
Thelma Lee
Ft. Worth, Tex.

Chapter 3

A Doctor Speaks Hebrew
by the Holy Spirit

A common misconception held by many critics of speaking in tongues has been that it happens only to the uneducated, emotionally unstable people who have abnormal personalities. The facts are that men and women in all walks of life and all manner of professions have received the experience. Here is the testimony of a well-known Christian surgeon in Jacksonville, Florida.

August 1, 1972

Editor: *New Wine* Magazine

Dear Sir:

In a recent issue of your magazine, a request was made for testimonies concerning the operation of the gift of tongues in the lives of Christians.

About a year ago, I was flying from Jacksonville to Mobile, Alabama, to speak for the Full Gospel Business Men's Fellowship. In the course of the flight we landed in Pensacola, Florida, and the pilot announced that the flight would be indefinitely delayed because of two flat tires. I departed from the plane with the idea of renting an automobile to drive into Mobile. As I was in the process of renting a car, a well-dressed lady came to the counter and asked for some keys to an automobile she had just driven over from Mobile. She turned to me and said, "Would you like a ride to Mobile?" I replied yes, and followed her out of the terminal. On the way out she said she wanted me to know it was definitely not her policy to take hitchhikers! I told her I understood her position, and added that I felt Jesus had had her drive over to pick me up. She received this as a friendly jest and we drove away.

During the course of our fifty-mile trip she related her life history to me, telling me that she was a Jew of Jews and how she had been told about Jesus in her Temple. She also related the problems in her life; how she was a widow with a large business and had several children with problems. God began to show me the needs in her life and began to impress me with a message in an unknown tongue which seemed to be for her.

I was concerned that this be in God's order and timing so I asked the Lord to give me "the gap in her armour." The Spirit impressed me to ask her if she enjoyed praying. At that she responded with open joy and began to tell how she loved to pray. I then told her that her "Elder Brother" could teach a person how to worship God in another language and then I began to speak the words of the message God gave me. By this time we were driving into Mobile, along the waterfront where the Battleship Arizona is berthed, and this lady was obviously visibly moved by the strange words I spoke.

She turned to me and said, "How do you know Hebrew?"

I related to her that I did not know any other language than English and that to me the words were of unknown meaning. She then said, "You just told me in Hebrew that as a daughter of Zion I must stop and seek God." She continued by saying, "I know now that I really do love Jesus Christ." She then drove me to the hotel and went on her way.

In Jesus' name,
W. Douglas Fowler, Jr., M.D.
Jacksonville Beach, Florida

Chapter 4

Glossolalia in Welsh

Rev. H. A. Maxwell Whyte has been pastor of the United Apostolic
Faith Church in Scarboro, Ontario, Canada, for over twenty years. In
addition to his local pastoral ministry, he travels widely, speaking on a
variety of Christian themes related to the deeper Christian life. He is the
author of a number of books including, *The Authority of the Believer,
Pulling Down Strongholds, Dominion Over Demons* and *The Emerging
Church.* The following testimony was sent to me in a personal letter
from the Rev. H.A. Maxwell Whyte.

In 1944 I was stationed in Hereford, in the west of
England, and fellowshipped with the local Apostolic Church.
One of the elder brethren named Frank Hodges told me the
following story, and I can vouch for its absolute truth. Frank
Hodges was one of the Apostolic Church's most outstanding
pastors and a man of impeccable honesty.

In about 1910 Frank Hodges was walking along, talking
with the Lord, in a South Wales mining town. This was just
after the great Welsh Revival and at the beginning of the
Apostolic movement which succeeded it. The voice of the
Lord seemed to speak to him, saying, "Go up that mountain
and take the man who is coming toward you with you."

Frank Hodges glanced up and saw a stranger approaching
him, so, in obedience to the Spirit he said, "Sir, God has just
told me to walk up this mountain and to invite you to go up
with me."

The man replied, "I do not know you and God has not
told me so I am not coming." Thereupon, brother Hodges
started to be obedient to the voice of God himself. As he

began to ascend the mountain the other man suddenly came after him saying, "The Lord has told me to follow you."

They finally arrived at the top. (South Wales is full of mountains that fall down to the sea.) Once at the summit, Frank Hodges felt impelled to speak in tongues as the Spirit gave him utterance. As he spoke and the other man listened, two more men arrived at the summit from the other side of the mountain and they also listened.

When the speaking in tongues was finished, one of the two men exclaimed, "How did you know?"

"Know what?" Brother Hodges asked. Then the man explained that he had been telling in detail the story of the immoral life of the man who had reluctantly accompanied him up the mountain.

The tongue spoken was pure Welsh as was spoken in those mining towns, yet Brother Hodges explained on question that he knew not a word of Welsh. But by inspiration of the Holy Spirit he had said that the man was living in an immoral association with a girl in a nearby village, that he was not a Christian but God wanted him to become one.

All this was understood by both the men who had ascended the mountain from the other side and by the man who had accompanied Hodges. The two men were astonished and questioned Brother Hodges about how he knew such details. Hodges explained that he had spoken in tongues as the Spirit of God had enabled him, but that he himself was not only ignorant of the tongue but the contents!

The two men then said, "Would you be willing to come to the village and this girl's home and tell *her* what you have just told us?"

Brother Hodges replied he was willing to accompany them and to speak to the girl, but that what came out would have to be of God and he could not guarantee he would speak in Welsh again! So they went down the mountain to the village and entered the girl's cottage. Again Frank Hodges began speaking in Welsh; this time the message unfolded the immoral life of the girl. It told how she was living in sin with the man who was present with them in the cottage, that she should repent of her sin, and get right with God. He said God would forgive her and that she and the man should be honourably married.

The girl understood, confessed her sin and fell on her knees and gave her heart to the Lord. The man, seeing what was happening and the miraculous source of it all, also fell to his knees and cried out to God for mercy, and they were both converted to Christ in that cottage in South Wales.

No wonder Paul says, "Tongues are for a sign, not to them that believe, but to them that believe not" (I Corinthians 14:22). Perhaps we need more speaking in tongues and less evangelistic gimmicks to win the lost to Christ.

H.A. Maxwell Whyte
Toronto, Canada
Nov. 5, 1972

Chapter 5

Peace, The Messiah Is With You

Reverend Edward J. Sweeney is a former Roman Catholic priest now engaged in fulltime charismatic ministry. I have had the privilege of ministering with Rev. Sweeney and found him a gentle, dedicated minister of the word of God.

June 23, 1972
Dear Don:

Enclosed is a testimony from my own life, attesting to the validity of the gift of speaking in tongues. If it will redound to the Glory of the Lord and you are led to use it in the book which you are writing, please feel free to do so. I thank the Lord for you, your ministry, and the testimony of your life.

During the last week of August 1971, I was privileged to attend my first Tennessee—Georgia CFO. I am a clergyman and had resigned from my parish work in February of the same year. The experience which I had at this Christian camp was one of the most beautiful of my entire lifetime. I had received the Baptism in the Holy Spirit on June 17 of 1970 but I had never had such a strong personal confirmation of the supernatural character of speaking in tongues. The Lord had blessed me often in the past with a myriad variety of languages in my private devotional use of tongues. At times I seemed to be able to recognize, by sound, certain languages such as German or Spanish. On the last night of CFO, Friday, August 27, as I was standing in front of the auditorium after the evening service, I saw a young man standing a few feet away from me. I recognized him as the last person whom I had baptized the day before. He was wearing around his neck a chain on which hung a cross and a Star of David. I walked over to him and told him that I wanted to meet him since I had had the privilege of baptizing him. He told me that his name was David. I asked him if he was a completed Jew, and he said, yes, that he had accepted Jesus and was filled with the Holy Spirit. We chatted a bit and then he proceeded to tell me that I had been an instrument of real blessing to him during the week. He asked if I remembered him sitting next to me at a prayer meeting which I was leading on the previous Wednesday. I said, "No, I don't remember you being there."

Then he proceeded to share with me that he had been torn and racked with a great deal of doubt and confusion about his relationship with Jesus at that particular time, and that during the meeting as I was quietly praying in the Spirit he heard in perfect Hebrew, the following words come from my mouth: "Peace, the Messiah is with you." At this moment, he said that a tremendous peace settled over him and he felt the presence of the Lord.

As he related this simple and beautiful incident, of which I had no previous knowledge, a few tears slowly began to stream down my face and I was deeply moved at how sovereignly God works and how much he cares for every one of his children. I then, perhaps more out of curiosity than anything else, asked him to listen to my prayer language and see if it was Hebrew that I was speaking at this time. He said no that it was not Hebrew but he was quite certain it was another Semitic language because he recognized certain roots that were the same as the Hebrew language.

Every time I recall this incident, I am deeply moved and praise God for the proof of being used in this way and confirming to me the genuineness of this so-called controversial gift. "Every good gift and every perfect gift is from above, and cometh down from the Father of lights, with whom is no variableness, neither shadow of turning." [James 1:17]

With this simple and beautiful intervention of the Lord in David's and my own life, the above Scripture was quickened to me and the dispensational theology which I had learned in seminary days — claiming that glossolalia and the other gifts ceased at the end of the Apostolic Age — was forever disproven to me.

Praise the Lord!!

Sincerely in Christ Jesus,
Rev. Edward J. Sweeney
Atlanta, Georgia

Chapter 6

Why It Is, I Do Not Know

This testimony is one of several I have received in which identified tongues, rather than convincing the one recognizing them, serve primarily as confirmation of God's presence and power to strengthen the faith of the one praying.

March 6, 1972

Dear Don Basham,

Greetings in the name of Jesus Christ our Savior. I have had a unique experience regarding tongues; at least I have never read of an experience quite like it.

I was saved in a Baptist church in La Puente, California, in 1957. In 1958 I received the Baptism in the Holy Spirit at the Full Gospel Business Men's Convention in Los Angeles. My tongue speaking came word by word over a period of months and years. In fact, God still supplies many new words at different times.

After my experience in Los Angeles, I traveled considerably, finally settling down in Santa Fe, New Mexico, where I taught school for a period. Then I applied for a position of educational director with the Pueblo Indians of northern New Mexico. I was employed by the Indian Community Action Agency and thoroughly enjoyed working with the Indian people.

Part of my responsibility was to make occasional visits to eight different pueblos located many miles apart in northern New Mexico. The eight pueblos were: Teseque, Pojoague, Nambe, San Ildefonso, Santa Clara, Picuirs, San Juan, and

Taos. My primary responsibility was to provide sound educational training at each pueblo. This made it necessary for me to meet with each pueblo's council (a group of older men who directed the affairs of their pueblo).

It was at one of these meetings at Taos that the unique thing to which I refer took place. As I stated, the men on the councils were generally the older men of the pueblo, many of whom did not speak English. While I was sitting with the men in the council chambers waiting for the meeting to start, I was listening to their conversation. They were speaking in their native language, Tewa. As I listened I began to recognize certain syllables as identical to those I used when speaking in tongues. I finally became bold enough to ask the Indian next to me to listen as I spoke to see if he could understand anything that I said. He replied that he would.

I began to speak in tongues. (Actually, I was praying in the Spirit, seeking God as always.) When I concluded, a few moments later, I asked him if he understood anything I had said. He replied, "Part of it."

I asked which part and what did it mean. He repeated one phrase I had spoken and told me it meant, "Why it is, I do not know." I asked if he had understood any other words I had spoken and he replied, "No, but it sounded like Apache."

I have never visited any Apache Indians to inquire if it might be their language, but I have since marvelled at God's greatness and His leading in allowing me to know once again that speaking in tongues is real.

Respectfully yours,
Stanley Lamb
Sayre, Oklahoma

Chapter 7

Kun Meh, How Come You Pray in Perfect Thai?

When my first book *Face Up With a Miracle* was published back in 1967, one of the very first responses I received came halfway around the world from a missionary in Thailand. Her letter stated how my book was helping in the promotion of a spiritual revival on the American Air Force base near Udorn, Thailand. I was so deeply moved to realize that suddenly my ministry was having an affect in ways and places I never dreamed it could that I never forgot that letter nor the missionary who wrote it.

Later I met Mrs. Nina Miller, the missionary who wrote me. Now it is a distinct pleasure to be able to include this letter from her, testifying to a miraculous experience with speaking in tongues in Thailand.

May 29, 1972

Dear Don Basham,

You may remember me for I wrote you from Udorn, Thailand, when conducting a servicemen's center there, after reading your book *Face Up With a Miracle.* Last summer, shortly after I returned from Thailand, I met you personally at your meeting in the Community Baptist Church in Topeka, Kansas.

Today, here in Plainview, Texas, where I have been sharing our experiences in Thailand, I picked up a copy of the February issue of *New Wine* magazine and saw the notice that you wanted testimonies of Spirit-Baptized Christians who had experienced speaking in a recognized and identified language. May I share my experience with you?

It was while conducting the servicemen's center in Udorn, Thailand, that I was given a small ministry with some Thai people. I had prayed with two Thai women who could speak very limited English. I was praying for them to receive the

Holy Spirit. Later, they brought another Thai woman — one whom I knew was an earnest, born-again Christian, Mrs. Bon Johne — and asked me to pray for her. She knew no English at all and I know so few words in Thai that I asked a Christian government official who spoke fair English to interpret for me.

I explained Luke 11:13 to the woman and told her how to receive the Baptism by faith when I laid hands on her and prayed. Since all the people in the room were Thai and understood so little English, I prayed for her first in English, then slipped into praying in my own prayer language. Immediately she raised her hands and with tears streaming down her face she began to say with deep devotion, "Amen! Amen! Hallelujah! Hallelujah!" I knew God had met her need so I sat down to wait while she continued to praise the Lord with closed eyes.

At length she opened her eyes, looked at Mr. Tonsook, our interpreter, exchanging some remarks in Thai. Then Mr. Tonsook turned to me with a puzzled look on his face and asked, "Kun Meh, (Mrs. Mother) how come when I speak with you this morning you can only speak Thai *nitnoy* (very little), but tonight you pray for Mrs. Bon Johne in perfect Thai?" I was not aware of praying in the Thai language and I knew then that God had performed a miracle, for both Mrs. Bon Johne and Mr. Tonsook had understood me in Thai.

This experience came at a time when I had been asking the Lord if perhaps I should keep quiet about the tongues. I had my answer, and did not quench the Spirit as I had been tempted to do. If this testimony will help you in your book, I'll be glad.

Mrs. Nina Miller
Topeka, Kansas

Chapter 8

I Stand By
the Blood of Jesus

Many critics of tongues insist that the tongues on the day of Pentecost were known languages, which means they were altogether different from the tongues at Corinth, where the gift of interpretation was required. The Corinthian tongues were "unintelligible" at Corinth and required supernatural interpretation. But current experience has verified that at times speaking in tongues may be in a known language and still be interpreted supernaturally by someone not knowing the language, thus establishing that the tongues experience was the same, both at Pentecost and Corinth. This testimony is one such verification.

July 6, 1972
Don Basham
New Wine Magazine
Ft. Lauderdale, Fla.
Dear Brother Basham,

As I was reading last February's *New Wine* Magazine I came across an insert asking for testimony concerning the use of the gift of tongues where it was recognized as an authentic language. There is an incident in my own life which is, at least to me, a threefold testimony.

In the North Hills of Pittsburgh there are several rap sessions among Christians throughout the week. At the conclusion of one attended by a number of us, a young man in his late teens came to one of the elders of the group with a question about an experience he was having. In praying in tongues, one particular phrase kept coming to his lips over and over. He spoke the phrase and asked if it were really tongues. The elder suggested they pray for the interpretation right there and then. As they waited before the Lord, I listened very intently, for I had recognized the language as biblical Greek.

After a minute or so of prayer, the elder brought the interpretation. He said it meant, "I stand by the blood of Jesus." What I recognized from the Greek was, "I am established (stand, set) by (through, on account of, because of) the blood." The identification of Jesus was not in the Greek but was certainly in the context.

The tongue was thus established as a known language, the interpretation accurate (I know the elder knew no Greek) and the message itself one that would not come from an unclean spirit as some claim all tongues do.

You have my permission to quote, paraphrase, or otherwise use this testimony as you feel led.

In His Service,
Ronald A. MacDonald, Pastor
Gibsonia, Pennsylvania

Chapter 9

A History Professor Identifies Italian

May 22, 1972

Dear Reverend Basham,

Mrs. Sybil May Archer, whom you may know, asked me to write up my experience with a "known" tongue for a study that is being conducted in California. While this was underway, Mrs. Anna Blissit, whose name appears in the attached testimony, told me she had seen a notice in some magazine to the effect that you were also collecting examples of "known" tongues. She did not, however, recall the precise reason — whether for a book or something else.

Thus, without knowing whether what I have to say is at all appropriate for you, I am sending you a xerox copy of the testimony. I hope that it will help you in whatever project you are embarked upon.

Very cordially yours,
Philip E. Isett
The University of Texas at El Paso
Department of History

Gentlemen:

I understand that you are collecting specimens of glossolalia or speaking in tongues that are examples of known languages. I should like to add my own experience to those that you are receiving.

The following message in tongues was delivered to me in May of 1971 at the prayer meeting during which I received the Baptism in the Holy Spirit. It was delivered by Anna (Mrs. William N.) Blissit, an Episcopalian, who specifically stated to me afterward that she had no idea at the time what she was saying, nor even of what language she was using. The words were in Italian (a language I have studied) as follows: *Deo arondo, Sicco mondo.*

Mrs. Blissit was given to feel that this message was so important for me that, when she perceived that I was not paying proper attention, she grasped my left arm above the elbow and shook it.

The words constitute a promise of revival: "God is plowing the dry world," and were very important to me since I had had a strong concern for revival for at least five years. There are two principle points of philological interest concerning them; first the structure of the saying, and second the spelling that occurs in it.

Syntactically, three things are to be noticed, which, when taken together, give the words the distinctive structure and flavor of an Italian apothegm: 1) its form as a rhymed couplet (a common pattern for Italian sayings), combined with 2) the presence of a reversed noun-adjective combination, showing symbolic usage: *sicco mondo* rather than the usual *mondo sicco* 3) the omission of the definite article *il* in the second line. These usages are peculiar enough (though all are quite correct) to preclude their combined occurence in any phrase or saying made up by chance or by anyone not thoroughly familiar with Italian apothegmatic custom.

Orthographically, there appear two words which do not conform to the spelling of the Tuscan dialect that is the official Italian literary language, and which is taught in American schools. Instead of *Dio* we find *Deo,* and in place of *arando* the spelling *arondo*. One should notice that the latter spelling forms an integral part of the saying as a whole, since only the occurring variant will complete the couplet perfectly.

There are no specialists in Italian philology at U.T., El Paso, but I showed the words to Dr. Ed Blansitt of the Linguistics Department, whose specialties of study include Provencal (a language of the South of France). Dr. Blansitt said that the above vowel changes would suggest the saying to be couched in some North Italian dialect, though he could not name a specific one.

Very cordially yours,
Philip E. Isett
Instructor in Ancient and
Medieval History

Chapter 10

The Hands of the Master Speak

I once heard the testimony of a man who had attended a prayer meeting at a men's college dormitory in an Eastern city where the students were praising God in tongues. Suddenly one young man rushed to the corner of the room and picked up a small drum and began beating out a rhythm. The other Christians were concerned that he was "out of the Spirit" and that his drum playing was nothing more than an interruption to their prayer time.

But all at once an African exchange student with a room on the floor above burst into the prayer meeting exclaiming, "Who in here knows the drum language of my tribe?" Then he explained to the amazed group how he had recognized the drum beat and that the message had been words of praise to Almighty God.

Hearing the amazing testimony, I marveled at the wisdom and mercy of God who never limits Himself to do merely what man *thinks* He should do, but moves sovereignly to accomplish His own will and to glorify His own name.

The following testimonies are examples of yet another "Divine innovation" concerning the miraculous phenomenon we call speaking in tongues. With the permission of Mr. Lansing Gilbert, missionary secretary to the Deaf Evangelistic Alliance Foundation, we are including the following two testimonies. Those interested in knowing more of this unusual Christian enterprise may write to: The Deaf Evangelistic Alliance Foundation, R–1, Hastings, Michigan 49058.

A Miracle Sermon — Behind the unique Christian work among the deaf in the Orient lies a chain of acts of God preparing the way. Elsie Jaggers, sister and daughter of the Mother-Daughter Ada Coryell team reports this most unusual work of the Holy Spirit.

"Now I would like to go back a few years to an experience I think would just thrill you. That was when Ada herself, my sister, received the Holy Spirit and received God's call to the ministry of the deaf. She was "slain" under the power of the Spirit and was lying on the floor, when all of a sudden her hands began to form signs. Georgia, the wife of Sol Hoopi the famous Hawaiian guitar artist, was the pastor of a deaf church in Los Angeles and was sitting next to me in this assembly. All of a sudden tears began to stream down her face and she said, 'Elsie, do you know what Ada is doing?'

"I said, 'No, what is she doing?'

"Georgia replied, 'She is preaching in the sign language!' Then she began to interpret it to me. Oh! It was just beautiful. She was preaching an entire sermon — yet she did not know the sign language at all. This went on for two hours. She lay there preaching and even gave an altar call in the sign language.

"When she finally did get up, there was a deaf man in the service who was a sinner. He had never been saved but he knew Georgia, and after the service he went up to Ada and began talking to her in sign language. She just looked at him. She did not know what he was doing so finally he gave up and went over to Georgia and said, 'Sister Georgia, what in the world is wrong with that young lady? She was talking perfect sign language when she was lying on the floor, but now she acts as though she doesn't understand a thing when I talk to her in sign language.'

"Georgia said, 'Son, she doesn't understand. She doesn't know sign language.'

"He replied, 'But she was talking perfect signs!'

"Georgia shook her head. 'No, she wasn't — the Holy Spirit was!'

"Then, because of that miracle, the man knelt down right

there and gave his heart to the Lord. That was Ada's first deaf convert — when she was filled with the Holy Spirit.'

"Since that first miracle sermon, thousands of deaf people have been won to Christ through her ministry."

The Hands of the Master Speak — Many unusual stories have come from the ministry of the pioneer missionary team to the deaf in the Orient, Ada and Ada Coryell. That God is interested in the work among the deaf is confirmed by the many strange and unusual miracles that have followed those in the work. This wonderful story which happened during a brief visit of the Coryells to Pusan, Korea, illustrates the fact very effectively. In the words of the missionaries here is what happened.

"God has — where we couldn't get things clear — wonderfully helped the people to understand. While we were over in Korea holding meetings, a little Korean girl came to the services one day and listened to the story of Christ, and she made a decision to be a Christian but she did not fully understand. Some of the signs in Korea are different from those in Japan and Aimee Ada had only three days to learn the new signs.

"The little girl went home and said to herself, 'I don't fully understand, but I will pray because the missionary told me to.' So she knelt down and prayed before she went to bed. But still she said, 'I don't understand all I have done.'

"That night Christ appeared to her in a dream *and in perfect Korean sign language gave her the whole story of salvation and made her understand.* Then she got down on her knees and really repented of her sins and gave her heart to God. When she got up the next morning and told her parents what had happened, they were displeased and said,

'This little girl is not going to be a Christian!'

"They said to her, 'We are going to send you on a train to some relatives so you won't go to any more meetings.' However, she managed to slip away from her parents for a few minutes before leaving on the train. She came and told us the story of how God had made her understand. She testified that she was sure Jesus was in her heart.

" 'Now it doesn't make any difference,' she said, 'I still will tell others of Jesus and His love.' "

God has been so wonderful. Where we have failed, He has taken over. Later a letter from Korea revealed that a Christian Church had sprung up among the deaf there and they were hungry for more light.

Under the inspired ministry of the Coryell team, for the first time in any nation in history the deaf have their own church — nationwide — in Japan, all under deaf leadership. Since 1954 when there was a mighty outpouring of the Holy Spirit, the work has grown to be one of the largest protestant movements in Japan.

Chapter 11

The Strangest Conversation
I've Ever Been In !

Dear Don,

One Friday evening early in the fall of 1971, a group of Jesus People went to Fourth Street in Louisville, Kentucky, to witness to people on the streets. Fourth Street is the city's main thoroughfare and it was easy to find all kinds of folk there. We would approach an individual with a Jesus newspaper, ask for a donation and then ask if he knew Jesus. It didn't make any difference if the person was a hippie, a business man, a swinger, or a little old lady. We had learned to share the joy of Jesus with anyone who would listen.

We usually witnessed in teams, and this night I was with Leslie Ott and Molly Buskin of Louisville. All three of us are Spirit-filled and greatly enjoy the excitement of street ministry.

As we paused to catch our breath a moment, another girl, Kathie Ray, came walking up with a fellow who was chattering away to her in a foreign language. "David," she said to me, "would you talk with this dude? I've tried to talk to him about Jesus and I think he understands me, but he keeps coming back with this other language." I told Kathie we would try to get through to him so she left to continue her witness on up the street.

The young man turned to me and began to chatter in a language I did not know, but recognized as romantic. His characteristics led us to believe he was of Spanish (Latin) background. As he talked, he made points on his fingers and it was obvious he was directing a message to us. We stood and smiled at him, wondering what to do.

After several minutes of this unfruitful communication, I said to Leslie that I guessed we had nothing to lose, and with that I turned to the young man and spoke to him for a moment in my prayer tongue. I was amused by the apparent absurdity of the situation for I did not understand what he had said, nor did I know the language I was speaking.

I was astonished then, when he looked at me rather intently and spoke again in his language, then paused as if waiting for me to say something more. I did. I spoke more words in my tongue, making the message a little longer than the first one. Again he responded with a spiel in his language.

With this, the girls, amazed at what they were seeing and hearing, encouraged me to continue speaking with him in my prayer language. The young man and I conversed with each other for the next three or four minutes. This was the strangest conversation I'd ever been in! Obviously, he was understanding me and commenting on what I would say, while I was just talking (praying) in the Spirit and not comprehending a word either of us said.

I finally thought I had better try to end the session, so I asked the man in English if he understood our language. He said, in broken English, he understood English and could speak it somewhat. He related that he was in the army, stationed at Fort Knox, Kentucky, and that he had been raised in Puerto Rico.

We told him that what I had said was spoken in tongues and that I had no mind knowledge of what I had said. He listened to this explanation with much interest and told us that he knew of the gift of speaking in tongues but he had never before heard it.

He went on to say that my tongue was an academic dialect of Spanish that could be understood by any Spaniard, Mexican, or Puerto Rican. He said I had spoken it fluently and flawlessly. As he said these things my spirit was bubbling and my mind was rebelling. To the natural man, what was transpiring was folly; but to the spiritual man, it was edifying.

One of the girls asked him to tell us what had been said. He replied that my words had been directed to his relationship with Jesus. The Spirit had said through me that at one time he and Jesus had walked very closely, but he had turned his back to Christ and his heart had grown cold. If he wanted to find his life and happiness restored, I had said, he would have to return to Jesus and open his heart to Christ's purifying love.

When I heard him tell me what I had been saying in the Spirit, I was very moved. I knew we had witnessed a modern miracle on the main street of a thriving twentieth-century city.

There was little more we could say to him in English, for the Spirit had witnessed to him with the words he needed most to hear.

D. David Dyke
Louisville, Kentucky

Chapter 12

Hail the King Jesus!

March 6, 1972

Dear Brother Basham:

I read your ad in the February issue of *New Wine* magazine and I would like to help you in anyway that I can. We have had quite a move of the Spirit here in Florence, as people are experiencing everywhere as God pours out his Holy Spirit.

I have a Prayer and Praise Meeting at my house every Tuesday night, and the Lord has moved among us with such great power and has baptized many people in his Holy Spirit. We have also had many of the gifts of the Spirit manifest at our meetings. One night we had seven people receive the Baptism with the evidence of speaking in tongues. Praise God and to Him be all the glory! After this night I couldn't even sleep.

Each week we have had people receive the Baptism and I praise the Lord for what he is doing. We like to give the people a chance to come together and exercise the gifts of the Spirit. God really moves when His people come together and praise Him.

One night we had a man named Danny receive the Baptism and start speaking in tongues while a lady was present who had grown up in the Catholic church and had learned Latin. The language that Danny was speaking was perfect Latin and he had never learned or studied Latin before. She translated

62

everything he said and it was so beautiful! From this experience there were several more who received the Baptism. This was an answer to prayer and it really thrilled and humbled us before the Lord. Praise God. I cannot remember all, but some of what he said was, "Glory be to God, Praise God, Praise God. God is almighty, God is omnipotent, Praise and Glory be to God. Hail the King Jesus, Hail the King Jesus! Jesus is lifted up as Lord of Lords and King of Kings." There were many more things that were said but I can't remember them all.

I hope that this information will be of some help to you in bringing glory to the name of the Lord Jesus Christ. If I can be of any more help to you please let me know. May God richly bless you and your ministry.

Love in His Service,
Bubba Grimsley
Florence, S.C.

Chapter 13

Obtained the Victory Alone

November 15, 1971
Dear Pastor Basham,

My sister, attending a seminar in Pittsburgh, Pa., the week of October 15, talked to you about my story, and told me you expressed interest in the details for your new book. You have my permission to use the story, or any part of it, along with my name, if you so desire.

I am a housewife and mother of a fourteen-year-old daughter and a son age nine, and am a Lutheran by faith. I feel what makes my story more of a miracle than some is the fact that I never attended a prayer meeting prior to my Baptism in the Holy Spirit, so I had never heard anyone speak in tongues. Therefore there was no chance for me to imitate or copy anything. All I had was the Holy Spirit instructing me.

Sometime in November of 1970 I started reading my first book on the subject of the Baptism in the Holy Spirit. It was the book *Face Up With a Miracle* by Don Basham that inspired me first, and especially the chapter I call the do-it-yourself chapter. After finishing the book I felt a desire to be alone, so I locked myself in the bathroom. I was feeling a tingling sensation on the tip of my tongue and felt it might be the Holy Spirit. I uttered a few strange sounds and within a few seconds I had been given a spiritual language, more fluent and rapid than my own language. It was so easy and felt so natural I almost doubted if it was from God. But deep down I knew I had experienced what the people had experienced in the book I had read. The release and joy I experienced were beyond describing. For three days everything looked more beautiful to me — the shrubbery and the grass looked greener, and my children looked more beautiful to me. As I used my new language it seemed I could pray for only three things:

1. Total commitment to Jesus.
2. To see others through Jesus' eyes.
3. To be filled with the Spirit of Jesus.

This happened to me on a Wednesday and two days later I drove to Harrisburg, Pa. to meet my husband at the airport. As I drove along praying in my new language, my mind would flash with thoughts of how I could ever begin to explain the experience to my husband. You see, he was even more of a thoroughbred Lutheran than I was, having gone to a Lutheran college. Several weeks later I did share my experience with a close friend, but not until the next June did I feel it was time to share my experience of the Baptism in the Holy Spirit with my husband.

I kept reading more and more on the subject, mostly the articles and books my sister gave me, but did not use my new language very much until about June of 1971, when I began to pray in tongues almost daily. One phrase seemed to be stressed very strongly by the Holy Spirit, so I wrote it down on paper the way it sounded. The phrase and the way it seemed to spell was "Mon na nee ka." I know very little about separating syllables with the proper accent marks, but I felt this was very nearly accurate, and also knew beyond any doubt it was a word or phrase which had meaning.

On the second of June, 1971, I decided to call Basil Grapsas, a Greek friend of ours who was educated in Greece and had been in the United States less than ten years. I asked him if the phrase had any meaning to him. I did not tell him why or how I heard the phrase, but he explained it the following way:

Mon means one; add the *e* to *mon* and it means she or female. Then, *niki* or *neka* (either way is correct) means victory. So he said it would be written *mone niki* and gave me the translation for it: "Obtained the victory alone." What sentence or message could be more fitting for me, as I remembered being by myself in the bathroom with no one around to instruct me or guide me. I cannot remember any day of my life as being happier!

Now I realized it was time to share with my husband and family the events that had taken place in my life for the past seven months. I honestly feel the main reason I was provided the interpretation of the phrase in tongues was for proof to my husband. It was the Lord's way of breaking through his scientific mind. Since a mutual friend who knew the Greek language could translate a phrase I had heard in my mind and had pronounced and spelled almost perfectly, it surely had to be a gift from God!

Jesus has moved in and blessed my family and relatives in many ways this past year. My husband and children have received the Baptism in the Holy Spirit and there have been many healings in my immediate family. Isn't Jesus wonderful?

It is sufficient to say that before all this, in spite of my lifelong membership in the church, I did not know God. Up until this time I had a head full of theology but nothing in my heart. I had never felt the real presence of Jesus, nor had I ever been touched by Him. The only way I can describe it is to say it was as if I had a television set, but until I inserted the plug and put up an antenna to make contact, it was a dead and lifeless piece of equipment. Now I feel so alive and free, and know beyond any doubts that Jesus is alive!

Yours in Christ,
Orpha M. Kauffman
Lewistown, Pa.

Chapter 14
When Did You Learn
To Speak Syrian?

April 10, 1972

Dear Mr. Basham:

I receive the *New Wine* magazine regularly, and continually thank our Lord for the Spirit-led staff. I noticed your ad concerning persons who have had the experience of speaking in other tongues. My friends also called me and hoped that I would relate my happening.

I was a professing atheist from about 1963 until April of 1970, when I accepted Jesus. But God saw the hunger in my heart and sent a neighbor's son to give me the opportunity of turning my life over to Christ. He had been the original *Peck's Bad Boy,* joined the army, was in Berlin at the time of the Scandinavian airlift sponsored by the FGBMFI. He was saved and filled with the Spirit at the same time. On leave, he followed the urging of the Holy Spirit and came over to our house to witness. It took me until September of that same year before I felt ready to receive the Baptism, but I finally did.

Ten days later, my husband and myself went to visit a former friend who had moved away from New Castle. I went armed with the Bible, intending to witness to his wife who had been a Christian but had married a Muslim and become backslidden (I was sure). When we arrived, it was the husband, Fred, who exclaimed at my carrying the Bible. It turned out that he had been exposed to Christians over the last five years, being in and out of hospitals, and had read the Bible five times! We talked for an hour or so, when I felt the, as we say, anointing, and just had to speak out what was forming in my throat. After speaking for several minutes, actually I can't estimate how long, I looked at Fred and he was crying, and said to me, "When did you learn to speak Syrian?" I cannot speak Syrian, only English and Hungarian. He knew I couldn't have learned it in the years that I hadn't seen him. He said I spoke in beautiful, clear Syrian, holding him up to God to be healed. He had cancer of the bladder; I immediately asked him if he wanted to accept Christ as his Savior. He said, yes, yes! He prayed the sinner's prayer, and we had a wonderful time that afternoon reading Scriptures and talking about the Holy Spirit. He knew he had had a visitation from God, and did not turn away from the opportunity to accept Christ. He died six weeks later, and we know he is in heaven now, because I obeyed the Holy Spirit.

If you have any questions, please feel free to write, and I will do all I can to assist you in areas you may want to clear up.

Sincerely,
Rose Robertson
New Castle, Pennsylvania

P.S. So far, this is the only time I know that I spoke in a language used on earth.

Chapter 15

I Recognized That Language !

One of the truly amazing phenomenons of our time has been the opening of many Jewish hearts to the gospel of Jesus the Messiah. There is an increasing hunger in the hearts of many of God's chosen people to hear the truth about Jesus. Some who formerly spat in the dust at the sound of his name now openly ask, "Can he be the Messiah, after all?"

Here is the story of a completed Jew who has returned to Israel to live his faith and to help in the spiritual awakening among his people. We are reprinting his testimony and portions of the letter which accompanied it.

March 29, 1972

Dear Brother Basham,

I heard you speak once and know the Lord is with you in your work for my Messiah. I also heard about your request for testimonies about known tongues and am enclosing a tract of mine.

I'm here in Israel by faith since February . . . . The Lord has told me to be wise, and I hope to reach the Jews. Here we are not missionaries, but witnesses, and we are not converted but completed. I'm a new Jew.

By faith we will try to build a platform for the Jewish believer here in Israel. I have no one behind me here or in the U.S.A., but I have God. It is truly a miracle how the Lord has helped us and we thank him from the bottom of our hearts. Since I became a believer much has been against me, but now

I know it was all preparation for coming here. Thank you for praying for us.

Donald M. Leidmann, M.D. Ph.D.
Beverly Hills, Calif.
and Jerusalem, Israel

A New Heart Without a Transplant — (The Donald Leidmann Story) I was brought up as an Orthodox Jew, born on "the green side of the fence," never having known want for anything. Our home was in Sweden.

Very early in life there was within me a great longing to become a medical doctor, and I was very persistent about it. My father did not look with favor upon my choice, but strangely enough, it was the study of anatomy which finally brought me to God. The human body with all of its intricate checks and balances is truly a miracle, and the Genesis record told me it was created in God's image.

After completing medical school and following a few years of practice in Sweden, I told Father of my desire to go to the United States. However, to satisfy him, and because he so strongly urged it, I continued six more years in the university to complete my master's degree in civil engineering and obtain a Ph.D. in economics.

The Dead Sea Scrolls — Sweden being a neutral nation during the Second World War, I volunteered for six months in the air force. After the war, and following the discovery of the Dead Sea Scrolls, I asked permission to go to Jerusalem that I might read them. Two archeologists who had studied the ancient Aramaic, the old Hebrew Scriptures, and even the ancient Egyptian language, accompanied me. I had been such a doubter, wanting to see and prove everything first before believing it, and there I saw the original writings of the prophet Isaiah that pointed directly to a new covenant to come.

Studying the Old Testament and then following through logically to the New, I began to realize that there was indeed a new covenant that came after the old covenant from Sinai. That is something Orthodox Jews do not accept. Study revealed that the new covenant didn't cancel the old one, but rather fulfilled it. Although I was not at that time a Christian, and did not become one until many years later, reason and logic told me that the New and the Old Testaments must be taken together.

Upon returning home in 1954 from my third period of study in Jerusalem, I told my father it was no longer possible for me to live in hypocrisy and refuse to accept the plain facts of which my studies had completely convinced me. Disowned by my family as a result, I came to America.

A Messenger From God — Some years later, as I lay in a Seattle hospital with a very serious heart attack and a bleeding ulcer, it seemed this was the end of the line for me. God in His mercy, however, sent one of His messengers to effect my deliverance. In the bed next to mine, in the intensive care room, lay another man who spoke Swedish. We talked a little in that language, then he began to tell me about Jesus. At first I listened politely, but finally I told him I didn't believe that Jesus was the Messiah, and requested that he leave me alone.

He didn't stop talking about the Lord, however, and I soon discovered that he attended a local assembly in Seattle. When he couldn't get anywhere with me, he told his daughter and her husband and they began to talk to me about Jesus.

Although this displeased me, and I told them I didn't want to listen, they added insult to injury by laying their hands on my feet and praying for my recovery.

A New Heart — That night I slept soundly for the first time in many nights and awakened the next morning feeling like a million dollars. My breathing was easy and there was no more pain.

The doctor came in and remarked on how well I looked. I told him I felt fine and wanted to get out of there. He had anticipated my hospital stay would be at least six months, but upon my insistence, he consented to a checkup and another EKG. After looking at the tape he asked, "What's wrong with this machine? It says there's nothing wrong with your heart!" Forty-eight hours later he ran another tape with the same result. After a few days a third EKG proved there was nothing wrong with my heart. I was also healed of my bleeding ulcer, and after nineteen days I was released.

As a medical man I *knew* one does not get a new heart overnight — unless it's a transplant. Logic began to put the facts together and my conclusion was that beyond the shadow of a doubt my recovery was of God. Immediately I thought of the Pentecostal church which my fellow patient attended, and decided I wanted to attend a service there. Reverend Wendell Wallace, a black pastor from Portland, Oregon, spoke that night, and it was there I found the Savior! Thus did God knock down my prejudices.

I Recognized That Language — During the International Convention of the Full Gospel Business Men's Fellowship in Beverly Hills, California, in 1968, my wife was most interested in attending the afternoon service when Kathryn Kuhlman was to speak. Although as a Jew I did not believe a woman should preach, to please my wife, we went. After about ten minutes I decided no woman was going to tell me what to do, so I said to my wife, "Let's get out of here and go shopping."

We went out and got into our car. As I started the engine, the radio came on and there again was the voice of Kathryn Kuhlman. I couldn't get away from it! She was praying for Demos Shakarian, the president of FGBMFI. As I reached toward the radio to turn it off, my hand stopped in midair. Brother Demos was speaking in tongues, in a language he had not learned, and I recognized that language! I had not believed in speaking in tongues. I spoke a number of languages myself, with my understanding, and I thought that was all there was to it. But Brother Shakarian was praying in ancient Aramaic — the language Jesus had spoken — and he was saying, "Dear Lord, I thank you for the years I have been privileged to serve you. Forgive me Lord, for the shortcomings that I have, and please let me serve you, even if I am a little man."

I Learned A Lesson — My spirit was so stirred that I began to weep, which was exceptional for me. Right there I learned a wonderful lesson — that God speaks through human beings today by the power of His Holy Spirit. Like Thomas the doubter, who was so melted to tears and belief when Jesus showed the wounds in His hands and side, my heart was softened. The tears flowed, and I believed. That evening we went back and told Brother Demos what had happened.

That same day God poured out His Holy Spirit upon me in a copious flood! It was a wonderful, glorious experience.

Since the Holy Spirit has filled my soul, I have seen many people — black and white, yellow and brown, Catholic and

74

Jew — filled with the Holy Spirit and I love them all. They are all my brothers in the Lord.

Chapter 16

A Sign to the Unbeliever

The man who has an experience has a distinct advantage over the man who has only a theory. To those of us who have personally experienced the miracle of tongues, the theories about what it really is or why it cannot be from God carry little weight.

By *experience* we know Paul was correct in saying "tongues are a sign . . . to them that believe not" (I Corinthians 14:22).

But Paul also said:

> If all prophesy, and there come in one that believeth not . . . he is convinced of all . . . and thus are the secrets of his heart made manifest; and so falling down on his face he will worship God, and report that God is in you of a truth.
>
> I Corinthians 14:24—25

So, prophecy can also convince unbelievers when it reveals their personal secrets. Even today, tongues, when identified, may contain a prophetic message which reveals the heart secrets of those who hear and understand.

In this chapter we are sharing two such testimonies: one published many years ago, and one which is current. The first is quoted from a booklet published by the United Apostolic Faith Church in London, England, titled *Speaking In Other Tongues* by Rev. James Brooke, pages 28—30.

"A certain Italian infidel in the United States, who was very, very critical, dropped into a Pentecostal meeting. He said to his friends, 'I am going down to see these fanatical people. They tell me they speak in tongues. I know four or five languages. I will tell you whether it is real or not.'

"He heard the preaching and responded to an invitation to kneel. A few yards away a young girl, twelve years of age, knelt, and as hands and hearts were lifted toward heaven, God began to move. This little girl broke out in a tongue and the man was fascinated. She swept on and on, paragraph after paragraph, chapter after chapter, in the Italian language.

"When the prayer was over, he rose to his feet confounded. He rushed over to a business man and said, 'Tell me, who was that young girl? How many languages does she know?'

" 'Well,' he said, 'she doesn't speak any language except English, unless the Holy Ghost gives utterance.'

"He went to another business man and received the same reply. Then he went to the young girl. 'Do you know what you were saying?'

" 'No,' she said, 'I didn't have the interpretation.' He had to acknowledge it was a picture of his life. It was all unfolded, chapter after chapter, from the time he went into exterminating, black, degrading sin — event after event, the happenings of days, weeks, months, and years, were gathered into a message of about forty-five minutes, and every word was as clear as day, every syllable perfect.

"The man went home, tossed on his pillow through the hours of the night under terrific conviction. He came back and God saved him. Later God filled him with the Holy Ghost."

The second testimony is contained in a letter from a Virginia housewife.

March 24, 1972
Dear Don:
I read with interest the article in *New Wine* that you are

collecting testimonies for a book. Perhaps you could use this one.

About two years ago, I was visiting a couple in their home and we began to talk about tongues. The wife had received the Baptism, but with only a few words in another language. The three of us began to discuss the experience. Tom, the husband, seemed very interested and asked many questions including: "Do you know what you are doing? Is it like a trance when you speak in tongues? Do you know what you are going to say?"

Tom, a stockbroker, has an investigating mind and usually wants proof before acting. Before this, he had asked the Lord for a definite sign or miracle. He would often say to us "I'm waiting for my sign." This particular evening, after he had questioned me at some length, he said "Speak to me in Spanish. I understand that." To be honest, this brought me up short. At this point I was not sure what to do. I didn't know Spanish in any way, shape or form. The only language that I had ever studied was high-school Latin.

With the thought, "Lord, it is your miracle," I said to Tom, "If you want me to speak in Spanish, you will have to ask Him."

He said, "Okay, Lord, let her speak to me in Spanish." Tom's asking the Lord directly himself relieved me of the responsibility for the failure or success of what was to take place. Well, I began to speak to him in tongues and *it was Spanish!* Beautiful Spanish, and Tom *did* understand!

I would speak a while and then say, "Tom, do you understand me?"

He would quickly say, "Yes, go on."

One peculiar thing — as I was speaking, I began to move

my hands in a pantomime, telling Tom about his childhood, his marriage, and a bit about his future. Interspersed in these sentences was what Tom said was "Tomaso, My Son" in Spanish. Now, during this I could not understand what I was saying myself, but the movements of my hands told a story that we could all understand. Yet, the secrets of his heart were kept locked. I always felt that this was Tom's so personally that his wife and I were allowed but so much insight. Our Lord will not expose our hearts to anyone but Himself. It would be too painful. This went on for approximately twenty minutes with me stopping now and then to make sure that he understood.

At this point, Tom has not made a full commitment to our Lord, but since He called him, "My Son," and this man has innate goodness, we know that it is only a matter of time before he comes to full stature of sonship. Until then, it is as the Scriptures teach us: it is a sign to the unbeliever (I Corinthians 14:22) and it does reveal the innermost secrets of the heart (I Corinthians 14:25). Tom has consented to the use of any or all of this testimony.

Please try to come back to Charlottesville soon. Free Union is only fourteen miles from Charlottesville. I work at Monticello (home of Thomas Jefferson) and would love to take you through.

In His Wonder,
Barbara McLaughlin
Free Union, Virginia

Chapter 17

I Wanted the Whole Chapel To Pray for Me!

As dedicated and talented teachers in the Ft. Lauderdale School System, Jim and Julia Chandler both find repeated opportunities for sharing Christ in counseling with their students. In addition, the prayer meetings in their home have resulted in many young people finding Christ and receiving the Holy Spirit. Here is Julia's testimony to an additional miracle of God.

April 14, 1972

Dear Don,

In answer to your request for personal testimonies about one's tongue being recognized as a real language, I would like to tell you about my experience.

I believe Jim and I shared with you and Alice how Jim received the Baptism in the Holy Spirit with tongues a year before I did, and how I fought him every step of the way. Then, about a year later we were serving as workers in a Methodist Lay Witness Mission in central Florida at which we constantly heard conversation about the Holy Spirit Baptism. When I heard that some very dear friends of ours, a retired pediatrician and his wife, were going to meet with a woman who has a ministry in praying for the Baptism, I decided to attend the meeting too. Before it was over (to cut a long story short), I had invited the whole chapel full of people to come to the altar and to pray for me to receive the Baptism — *with tongues!*

But as they laid hands on me, nothing happened — absolutely nothing! Then a friend, Glenda Miller, asked me to open my mouth and sing along with her. I was told later that it was a beautiful duet and that we sang syllable for syllable absolutely together. But that isn't the end of my story.

In spite of the fact that three weeks later both Jim and I experienced healing for our eyes so that neither of us has since worn glasses, I began to doubt the authenticity of my speaking in tongues. I was still singing the tune which I had sung with Glenda but I began to notice that God was giving me new words. Oddly enough, that made me doubt even more.

We went to Israel soon after that for another summer of study and travel. One day, in complete desperation, I got up and headed into the next room which served as the office of our young Jewish teacher-guide to ask him if the words I had been speaking in tongues meant anything at all or were they just a jumble of meaningless mouthings. I did not sing them, I just repeated them. To my utter amazement, he began to nod his head. "Julia," he said, "that's Aramaic. I teach it here at the school."

When I asked if the words meant anything at all he replied that loosely translated they meant, "I am the God who loves you, keeps you, and guides you."

Hallelujah! Praise the Lord! Don, I have *never* doubted the reality of speaking in tongues from that moment to this. God is so good!

He even gave me a second verification the same week. We were invited to dinner on the Mount of Olives where we met a charming and intellectual man and his daughter, also from the United States. I didn't have the remotest idea who he was, but listened enthralled as he told of his ministry in the Holy Spirit at a large church in New Jersey. When he was finished, I shared just briefly what had happened to me that week and he asked me to sing the song. Before I was halfway through he was nodding and said, "That *is* Aramaic. I teach it at Oral Roberts University." He was Dr. Howard Ervin, whom I'd read about in John Sherrill's *They Speak With Other Tongues.*

Need I say that Jesus and his wonderful provision of grace have grown sweeter with each passing day? What a tragedy that people refuse to acknowledge this provision and thus miss the power and blessing which could be theirs.

I thank God for the opportunity to share this testimony with others and pray that it will lead many to the reality of Jesus through this marvelous experience.

Your sister in Christ,
Julia Chandler
Coral Springs, Fla.

Chapter 18

You Men Are Angels
Sent From God!

John Cantrell works for a trailer manufacturer in Kewanee, Illinois. A Christian layman, he had been earnestly praying for the Baptism in the Holy Spirit for over two weeks. One morning, feeling blue and depressed, he was driving to work when the Holy Spirit graciously answered his prayer, then quickly confirmed that his experience was miraculous. His first letter of testimony describes what happened when he arrived at work; his second letter of testimony describes how God honored the witnessing ministry of John and his friends.

March 8, 1972

Dear Reverend Basham,

It was early in 1968, at noontime as I drove to work, that I first prayed in tongues. Arriving at my office still praising God, I found that Leonard Badal and I were there alone, both of us early for work.

With the tongues message still vivid in my mind, and knowing that Leonard was an immigrant from Iraq, I repeated a phrase and nonchalantly asked if he knew what it meant.

"Yes," he answered, "you said, 'Your Father (God) will grant you peace.' You spoke in Assyrian!"

So I repeated another phrase.

"Very good!" he exclaimed. "You said, 'Your Father (God) will take you by the hand and guide you through life.' You spoke Assyrian both times. Excellent diction! Where did you learn to speak like that? You spoke in ancient Assyrian, the mother tongue of all the Arab languages!"

John Cantrell

March 11, 1972

Dear Don Basham,

Here is a second tongues experience: It was in December, 1968, at 3:30 A.M. when Frank O'Hara, Tato Curet, and I left the all-night cafe at Indian Agency, Wyoming at the Montana state line. We were returning to our car when Frank noticed a car full of drunken Crow Indians. They were trying to start their car but their battery was dead. As we offered to push them, we could see men and women sprawled all over the inside of the car.

As we walked on toward our car, Wanda Medicine Horse jumped from the car and came running toward us.

"Oh, please help me, sirs! I'm going to be killed tonight!"

Wanda looked like someone had beaten and striped her face with a bicycle chain. On being told that Jesus can save to the uttermost, she said, "I know you can save me if you are Christians because it is Satan who is after me tonight."

Then Wanda asked to be driven to her sister's home to avoid her husband, Charlie Broken Rope. As we bounced across the dirt hills of the Indian reservation at her directions, Tato was in constant prayer as it seemed plain to us that strong evil forces were in the car.

Soon, even Wanda was praying and talking about Jesus.

"How disgusting," I thought, "that this drunken squaw woman should even speak the name of Jesus through her bloody lips!"

But as her praise to God approached true adoration it was clear to us that she had known Jesus at one time.

Stopping outside the home of her sister, we waited for her to get out. We were anxious to continue our trip, but Wanda asked us for prayer.

Frank O'Hara began to pray for her and soon was praying in tongues. Then he began what sounded like a strange gutteral chant. Frank wondered if perhaps the devil had taken hold of his tongue, so he stopped speaking.

"Oh, don't stop, " Wanda begged. "You are speaking to me in the Crow language!"

So Frank prayed again — first in English, then in tongues, and soon there came again this strange sing-song language. Wanda became very alert and very happy.

An amazed Frank asked, "Wanda, would you mind telling us what the Lord said to you?"

Wanda smiled, "You really don't know, do you? Well, for fifteen years I was a Christian and had served the Lord. During all those years I went to church services alone and had to face a beating from my husband upon my return home. Finally, I gave up, and for the past year I have not gone to church, but have simply gone along with the world's ways.

"Tonight, as God spoke through you, He told me He understands and is willing to take me back and use me. He said He would take me out of the mud and set my feet on solid rock and start me on a whole new walk in Jesus Christ! Now I know what heaven is like! I know that you three men are angels sent from God!"

John Cantrell
Kewanee, Illinois

Chapter 19

My Feet Haven't Touched the Ground Since!

March 3, 1972

Dear Mr. Basham,

I am writing about your recent request concerning tongues that have been acknowledged as a known language. I recently received my Master's degree in music and presently teach school. I gave a vocal recital in connection with my degree and sang three languages in this recital. I have sung at least five languages over the years and am studying voice with a Jewess who was born in Austria (her mother was an opera star there). She was educated in America and is a linguist. She teaches language and phonetics and can readily recognize many languages.

As a result of my receiving the Baptism in the Holy Spirit, I have been praying for deliverance for a weight problem, and through fasting and prayer God has delivered me. I had the conviction I should share my spiritual pilgrimage with my teacher, Mrs. Drucker, one morning at my lesson. She kept asking to hear more until I had shared my Baptism experience with her along with the fact that I had spoken in tongues.

She looked at me questioningly and said, "I have heard about that. Do you speak in tongues now?"

I answered, "Yes."

Right away she asked, "What does it sound like?"

I had been shy of speaking in tongues in front of people because I was still so new in the experience (eight months).

85

Then I remembered Father Dennis Bennett sharing that he always gave people the opportunity of hearing the heavenly language, so I began in faith, and God blessed me with at least a twenty-second message in tongues. When I finished I glanced at Mrs. Drucker. She looked awestruck and was rubbing her arms.

"Do you know what you were saying?" she asked.

I smiled, "No, I don't," never expecting to know.

"You were speaking Turkish!" she explained. "And I've got goose bumps going up and down my arms!"

Then I looked awestruck! "I was? Really?"

She then told me how her father-in-law had given them a Turkish poem a long time ago and how the family had repeated it over and over until they learned it. She repeated it to me and as she spoke I could recognize my tongue and I was so excited!

"How has your experience affected your children?" she wanted to know. Then I was really able to share with her about the gospel and about divine order in the home. It was a wonderful sharing, and as I continue to study with her this semester, I'm praying for more opportunity to share about my Messiah.

This whole thing happened to me only this past Monday and so you can imagine that my feet haven't touched the ground since! We are constantly amazed at how God is moving in our lives. We have been a part of meetings where amazing testimonies of deliverance and salvation have been shared. We praise God for His excellent greatness.

In the Name of Jesus,
Lois Quesenberry
Towson, Md.

Chapter 20

This Can't Be
Happening to Me!

The following testimony was provided by a personal friend, Miss Lee Kinney. Lee is secretary to Reverend Bob Mumford, a close friend and fellow Bible teacher.

March 8, 1972

Dear Don and Alice,

I noticed in *New Wine* magazine that you are looking for testimonies about tongue speakers who were understood. Well, you can add another fanatic to your list — me! It wasn't any real big deal, but it was an incident I won't forget. It happened like this:

While attending school at a most rigid, fundamentalist college in the Los Angeles area (Biola) I found the Holy Spirit quite active on campus. Having received the Baptism in the Spirit shortly before deciding to attend the school, I was anxious to see what the will of the Lord would lead me into while there.

It wasn't long before an interested group of students began to meet in a secret place on campus — a soundproof room in the music building. If someone felt inspired to pray or sing in tongues, no passerby would stop in to inquire — after all, folks were practicing in all sorts of languages in the same building, anyhow.

There were less bold students, however, who also became interested in all this "tongues business" (as it was so erroneously referred to). Knowing that speaking in tongues is such a thorn to so many dear evangelicals I preferred to de-emphasize it in consideration of those brothers and sisters in Christ. Taking this attitude paved the way into many tender hearts which had already been injured by other well meaning tongue speakers.

One of these shy sisters — we'll call her Marion — chose to speak to me about this phase of the Christian walk after dark, outside our dorm, while we were parked in my Volkswagen. Marion came from a long line of missionaries, having been born and raised in India herself. Her mom and dad were Christian Missionary Alliance missionaries deeply devoted to the Lord's work. (Why does it come as such a shock to some charismatics when we discover that an evangelical without the Baptism in the Spirit has a fervent love for God?)

As we talked quietly about the things of God, she decided to surrender to God for anything further He might have for her. As I prayed for her and we bowed our heads together, I had the feeling that I was being watched. I ignored the feeling and continued to pray in tongues.

After a short time it was too much for me — I couldn't resist peeking. Marion's eyes were as wide open as her mouth as she gaped at me. "What's the matter, Marion?" I asked, half holding my breath.

"It's what you said!" she replied. "I understood some of it; I knew what you were saying!"

I raised my hands to cover my face. Don't look shocked, I said to myself. Be blasé; act as if you knew all the time it was possible. Of course you'd heard of this. Why, there have been a number of big-name ministers who've been understood as they spoke in tongues. And the missionaries, too, remember?

The thoughts raced their way through my mind. But I'm

no minister, I argued to myself. I'm just a plain Baptist girl who received the Baptism in the Holy Spirit in someone's house. This can't be happening to *me!*

But I knew from Marion's face that it had happened. She tearfully explained that during her travels with her parents in the Middle East they discovered that in India alone there were over 180 languages and over 500 dialects spoken. Being familiar with the tenor of them and speaking a couple herself, she could get the gist of what I was saying. She noted that I was pleading with God for her. I had reminded Him that I was her sister, and He our Father, and that we would appreciate His grace in this matter.

My grateful heart overflowed as I joined her in speaking our heavenly languages together. Just two Christians praying together; two regular Christians — no one special — praying to a God who is *very* special, and who does all things well.

I might add, Don, how thankful I was later, as I reviewed the incident, that once a brother in the Lord had instructed us babes in the Spirit to attempt to be *articulate* in speaking in tongues, to endeavor to enunciate our languages in the event that they were known languages. I figured since the words were nigh me — even in my mouth — I'd do that from then on. I guess it paid off!

Bless you,
Lee Kinney
Hollywood, Fla.

Chapter 21

I Never Left You

March 17, 1972
Dear Don,

I was a homesick newcomer to Fresno, California, but I sought out a charismatic group and found Spirit-baptized Christians from all denominations meeting each Monday at the Full Gospel Tabernacle here in Fresno.

One Monday night, the teacher for the evening called for all who had needs to come to the front and stand. Then he asked all who felt they were living and walking in the Spirit to come and stand behind the needy ones and minister to them as the Spirit led.

I found myself standing behind a young woman. I couldn't see her face and she couldn't see mine. I prayed quietly in English first, then the Holy Spirit gave me such a compassion for whatever her need was, I began praying fervently in tongues.

Suddenly, she lifted her hands and also started praying in tongues. After a time of worshiping together she turned around and we talked.

She said she had been a Christian, had received the Baptism in the Holy Spirit and had even gone to Bible school. But then, for some reason she had strayed away from God and was trying desperately to get back to Him. She felt that she had messed up her life and had sinned so much He wouldn't take her back.

But as I was praying in tongues she understood what was being said (it was Spanish) and that the Lord had said to her, "I never left you, you left me, but I want you back. I've never stopped wanting you!"

And with that message her joy came back and she was able to believe and lift her hands and pray in tongues once more. She had been afraid she would never be able to do it again. She told me she was from Puerto Rico.

The Lord really blessed me through that experience and I've never felt homesick since.

Praise His Name!
Mrs. Lura McDannald
Fresno, Calif.

Chapter 22

The Young Woman Prayed in Swahili

Dear Mr. Basham,

I would like to share with you a testimony to the miracle of tongues that was witnessed by our Wednesday morning prayer group. At the time this occurred, we were a small group of newly Spirit-filled Christians who were very inexperienced in the ways of the Lord. We had recently committed ourselves to a weekly meeting for prayer and praise and Bible study. This particular morning the group was gathered in my home and we began the meeting as usual with some singing, after which a message in tongues came forth, followed by an interpretation.

A suggestion was then made that we offer some prayers of praise and thanksgiving. After several such prayers in English, one of our members (Shirley Stiller of Natrona Heights, Pa.) began praying in tongues. When she had finished we all waited expectantly, but no interpretation was offered and after a long silence the meeting proceeded as usual.

It was after the prayer time that a woman who was visiting the group, a missionary home on leave from Africa (Clara Rhines of Bukuria Mission, Kenya, E. Africa) spoke up.

"I don't know whether you know it or not," she said, "but the young woman who prayed a while ago was praying in Swahili." She then gave us the translation of the prayer which turned out to be just what had been requested; a prayer of praise and thanksgiving!

How good the Lord was to give us a sign to encourage us at that time and what a witness it turned out to be in the community to the power of the Holy Spirit! Praise the Lord!

Orie Montgomery
Natrona Heights, Pa.

Chapter 23

It Had to Be God

From 1964 to 1967, I was pastor of the East Side Church (Baptist-Disciples of Christ) in Sharon, Pennsylvania. During those years, I became friends with a pastor in nearby New Wilmington — Dr. Victor Dawe of the Neshannock Presbyterian Church. The town of New Wilmington is also the home of Westminister College, a small Presbyterian school. As a result of the charismatic ministry offered during Victor Dawe's ten-year pastorate at Neshannock church, a number of students and some of the faculty began to get involved in the movement of the Holy Spirit.

The weekly charismatic meetings in Neshannock church proved a source of great spiritual blessing, not only to many of its own members and to the college, but to a dozen or more area churches as well. One of my own members received a dramatic healing from glaucoma during one of the Saturday night meetings.

But as is often the case with ministers actively engaged in charismatic ministry, Dr. Dawe had his opposition — opposition which would eventually lead to the termination of his service to the Neshannock Presbyterian Church. One leading critic of his ministry was a retired missionary who was an active member of the church. The following letter from Victor Dawe relates the dramatic way God chose to convince this man of the validity of what was taking place in his church. I had heard others speak of this particular miracle of tongues and at my request, Dr. Dawe has provided a full account of the incident.

June 2, 1973

Dear Don,

Here is the information on the tongues episode involving the late Dr. J. V. Barrows, as corroborated by Dr. Joseph M. Hopkins of Westminister College. Dr. Barrows, a retired United Presbyterian missionary, was the teacher of an adult Sunday-school class and very active in the life of Neshannock church, when I received the Baptism in the Holy Spirit in 1964.

He was a very precious soul, a recognized "man of God," and solidly evangelical. But since he belonged to the old school, and because of some unpleasant experiences with Pentecostals on the mission field, he did not think very commendably about the Pentecostal experience. Yet I felt it was essential to have his support for my ministry at Neshannock.

Early in 1965, a number of us began to attend the meetings of the Youngstown, Ohio, chapter of the Full Gospel Business Men's Fellowship International. My good friend, Dr. Joseph Hopkins, who is sympathetic to the charismatic renewal, decided to invite Dr. Barrows to attend a chapter meeting with us. (I hadn't the nerve to invite him!)

After the dinner and the address by the speaker, those who were seeking the Baptism in the Holy Spirit and those who were to pray with them retired to an adjoining room. Dr. Barrows and Dr. Hopkins joined this group, purely as observers. My wife and I were also present.

The group formed a large circle, with Dr. Hopkins and Dr. Barrows sitting on one side, and my wife and I directly opposite. Sitting beside Dr. Barrows was a woman from Hubbard, Ohio, a housewife who requested prayer with the laying-on of hands. Two of the chapter officers came over to minister to her. As they prayed she began to speak in tongues, and as she spoke, I noticed there was one phrase which kept recurring.

When she had finished, Dr. Barrows turned to Dr. Hopkins and asked if she knew what she was saying. Joe Hopkins replied that he doubted if she did.

"But she's speaking Arabic and was repeating the phrase, 'The peace of God,' Dr. Barrows insisted. Then he turned and questioned the woman. Did she know what she was saying? Had she ever had any contact with the Arabic language?

Her answer to each of his questions was negative. She was just a housewife and could speak only English. She had never traveled abroad nor had she ever associated with anyone who spoke Arabic.

As Dr. Barrows and Dr. Hopkins talked further with her, they learned that two members of her family were mentally ill and that she had asked for prayer that they might receive the peace of God.

Once Dr. Barrows was convinced she was telling the truth, and that he had witnessed an authentic manifestation of the Holy Spirit, he raised his hand and requested permission to speak.

Since my wife and I were sitting opposite them, we had been unable to understand all that had taken place, but I did see Dr. Barrows' hand go up. I nudged my wife and said, "Watch this! Dr. Barrows is about to express his disapproval of what is taking place." (He was a forthright man and very readily and unapologetically expressed his convictions.)

But to my surprise, instead of criticizing, he began to apologize for the wrong attitude he had held toward the charismatic movement, and, citing the very incident he had just witnessed, said he was now convinced that it had to be of divine origin.

I do not believe that Dr. Barrows would have been convinced by just hearing an unknown tongue. I believe God had him attend that particular meeting and placed him beside that particular woman to hear her pray in Arabic so that he would be convinced of the authenticity of the experience and would feel led to support my ministry.

This he faithfully did for the seven remaining years of his life. His faithful support of my ministry continued to the end. Five months after his death, I was removed from the pastorate of Neshannock Presbyterian Church by action of the presbytery.

En Agape,
Victor Dawe
New Wilmington, Pa.

Chapter 24

How Kind of You To Pray for Me in My Mother Tongue!

This personal testimony is by a friend and close associate in ministry, Reverend Bob Mumford. Reverend Mumford is acknowledged as one of the leading Bible teachers in the charismatic movement today.

June 10, 1973

Dear Don,

Though I have had several experiences that could be categorized as unknown tongues being recognized, this instance is the most dramatic and easily described. It happened in a prayer group in Princeton, New Jersey, which meets in the home of Mr. and Mrs. P.A. Knudson.

There were about one hundred people in attendance, representing various denominational backgrounds, Presbyterians being predominant. Following a teaching session, a handsome and well-dressed man in his midtwenties approached me in the doorway between the dining and living room.

Visibly moved by the teaching, the praise and the presence of the Holy Spirit, he asked if I would pray for him. His accent was heavy, guttural and not easily understood. Before I could respond, he knelt in front of me. This was somewhat disconcerting and unexpected. Still, I laid my hands upon his head and began to pray in the Spirit.

He wept openly, and literally shook as I prayed. My subjective thought at the time was that my tongue was different, more guttural and German sounding than the one usually expressed through me. Secondly, I recall thinking, "The Lord surely loves this young man and is working in his behalf."

When I finished a short, rather ejaculatory and powerful prayer, he looked up and said, "How kind of you to pray for me in Hungarian, my mother tongue!"

Then the awesomeness of what had happened suddenly broke in upon both of us by some unspoken communication. He knew I wouldn't know Hungarian if I heard it and I knew that I didn't know what I had prayed (I Corinthians 14:14).

Further discussion revealed that I had prayed in a clear Hungarian language. The essence of what was said was that God had seen his fear and his faith; that God had not brought him through the multitudes of dangers in his own country and in this one only to forsake him at this time. Confidence in God's time and God's ability would reveal direction and placement which he would know was from the Lord. It is not difficult to imagine the overflowing joy in both of us as we realized the miracle in which we both had been partakers.

Bob Mumford
Ft. Lauderdale, Fla.

Chapter 25

How Great Is Our God!

April 8, 1972

Dear Brother Basham,

The following testimony is in response to your call in the February issue of *New Wine* Magazine. You may use it as you wish, to the glory of God. This incident took place several years ago in the First Christian Church of Vidor, Texas. My husband was the pastor there at the time.

Sandy is a member of another Christian Church, but the Lord graciously allowed us to lead her to a salvation experience and later into the Baptism in the Holy Spirit. She received the Baptism right in our own living room.

Later, she brought an out-of-town friend to our church. Sandy had led her friend Barbara to the Lord just the day before. Barbara was seventeen and a Baptist, and desired to learn more of the things of God. Our youth meeting was spent studying the Scriptures dealing with the Baptism in the Holy Spirit, then, some of our young people who were newly-baptized in the Holy Spirit, enthusiastically shared their experiences with her.

After the sermon that night she came to the altar (you can see this was an unusual Christian church) to seek the infilling of the Holy Spirit. My husband asked Linda, one of our fine young people, to pray with Barbara. Linda gave Barbara some instructions, as I laid my hand on her head and began quietly to pray for her in the Spirit. I noted at the time that the language of my prayer was rather slower and more distinct than usual.

After Barbara had beautifully received the Holy Spirit and had praised God in her new Spirit language, she looked at me in a rather puzzled manner and asked, "Am I supposed to understand you when you are talking in tongues?"

It was my time to be startled. "No," I answered, "not usually. Why? Did you understand me? And what did I say?"

Barbara told me I had spoken in Spanish, a language I do not know, and that I had prayed, "Dear God please give this saint the Holy Spirit."

When she said, "this saint," I knew that it was the Holy Spirit as I never use that particular term; in the natural I usually pray for "my sister" or "your child" or some such term. But the Holy Spirit, in His consistency, chose the same word he calls us in the Word of God. Praise the Lord!

Also, since I pray in several different languages in the Spirit, he chose the very one Barbara would understand. How great is our God! His ways are past understanding.

Sincerely,
Mrs. L. Guinn Busbee
Beaumont, Texas

Chapter 26

A Methodist Minister
Speaks Aramaic

July 25, 1972

Dear Brother Don,

Here's another testimony for your forthcoming book.

When I attended the Holy Spirit Teaching Mission conference in Ft. Lauderdale in the fall of 1970, I was in a prayer group when a Methodist minister spoke a sentence in tongues.

My nationality is Assyrian. Although I was born in Chicago, I learned to speak Syriac, which is modern Aramaic, from my parents.

Well, when this Methodist brother prayed, I recognized that he was speaking the Assyrian language and he was saying the names of the Father, Son, and Holy Spirit.

When I told him he had been praying in a real language, he was greatly blessed and encouraged, as we all were.

Yours in Christ,
John Booko, Pastor
Three Rivers, Michigan

Chapter 27

God Is Not Dead

When the word spread that I was seeking testimonies for this book, many friends came to my assistance by telling me of their friends who had such testimonies. One such couple was the Reverend Dick Coleman and his wife Mignon, of the Westside Baptist Church in Leesburg, Florida, who wrote that the testimony of their friends, Reverend and Mrs. Chester Coker, would be well worth printing. When I made contact with the Cokers, they not only agreed, but furnished me with an unpublished manuscript which contained details of the incident.

A striking feature about their miracle of tongues was that it contained prophecy concerning Reverend Coker's ministry, and, as the testimony dramatically shows, every statement in the prophecy was quickly fulfilled. Here is Reverend Coker's letter to me, followed by excerpts from the unpublished manuscript.

July 20, 1973

Dear Brother Don,

Thank you for your letter. We are glad to know that you are writing a new book and will be looking forward to *The Miracle of Tongues*. We were not aware that the Colemans had written to you about the experience which took place last year in our church, Trinity Tabernacle in Bushnell, Florida. We are sending you a manuscript in which my wife has recorded the events. You and your publisher have our permission to use this material in any way.

We pray for you and your ministry. If we may be of any further help, please let us know.

Sincerely in Christ,
Chester Coker
Leesburg, Florida

We arrived home from Korea still excited about the response and hunger we had found on the part of the Korean people to know the Lord. More people had been won to Christ during that trip than we had been able to win in over ten years in the pastorate in America. Little did we know that God was using that trip to prepare our hearts for an even greater call.

We came back to our church determined to see more of our own people won to the Lord. We decided to hold a series of special meetings and to schedule a number of outstanding speakers. My husband contacted Reverend Gerald Derstine from Gospel Crusades, Inc., Bradenton, Florida, about holding a meeting in our church. He was not free to come on the dates we requested, but told us of a pastor from the Philippines, Reverend C. R. Cortez, who was in the area and who might be able to minister in our church. So Chet wrote Reverend Cortez, inviting him to minister in our church in December. Brother Cortez later told us how he wrote Chet a reply, saying he could not come because of a previous commitment in the state of Nebraska.

He said he finished the letter about 9:30 P.M. and went to bed, intending to mail it in the morning, but during the night he had a vision of himself and a man he had never met, ministering together, and praying for another man. They were in a strange church and there was a circle of people around them, praying. When he awoke the next morning and started to mail the letter, God checked him and he could not mail it.

Then he sat down at the typewriter and found himself composing another letter: "Dear Reverend Coker, Please meet me at the bus station in Leesburg, Florida, at 9:00 A.M.

Saturday, December 11 . . . ." In the same letter he found himself inviting Chet to come to the Philippines to conduct nationwide crusades there. He later said evangelists from all over the country were asking him to set up crusades in the Philippines for them, but he felt led to ask Chet, even though he didn't know at the time that God had called Chet to be a missionary-evangelist.

When Brother Cortez arrived in Leesburg and met Chet at the bus station, he immediately recognized him as the man with whom he was ministering in the vision.

Meanwhile, our church had been spiritually prepared for Brother Cortez's coming. Many of our people had been periodically fasting, and the week before he arrived we had conducted five days of special services under the leadership of Reverend Dick Coleman and his wife Minnie, from the Westside Baptist Church in Leesburg.

On the very first night of the meeting, the anointing and leadership of the Holy Spirit was so sovereign that Brother Cortez abandoned his original plan to show films of his work in the Philippines, and the whole service was given over to singing and worshiping the Lord. Later in the meeting, he shared with our congregation his conviction that God was calling Chet to go to the Philippines and help evangelize his people. He asked my husband to kneel at the altar and invited people to gather around him and lay hands on him, praying that God's will would be done in his life. As we prayed, I felt an anointing from God to bring a message in tongues. As I spoke, tears began streaming down Brother Cortez's cheeks, and when I had finished, he explained that the message was in his native Ilocano dialect, and he had understood every word. It was a prophecy concerning my husband. This was the message:

> Yea, I say unto thee my son, if thou wilt humble thyself and obey My voice I will be with thee. And thou wilt go to the islands of the sea, and the brown race will receive blessings from thee and many shall come before thee to receive the Lord thy God and be filled with the Living Water. Many will be healed in the name of thy God and thy God will be with thee and supply all thy needs and use thee as a great vessel of blessing, saith the Lord.

Although the crusades in South Korea had taken all the money we could get together, in faith we began planning a trip to the Philippines. After conferring with Brother Cortez, we decided we would try to go during June and July, 1972, and, if the Lord so directed, to continue to South Korea for the month of August. We felt that our daughter Lisa, who was nearly seventeen, and our son David, who was nearly sixteen, should be involved in the ministry also. This meant the trip would cost approximately six thousand dollars. We had no money, but we believed God when He said, "Thy God will be with thee and supply all thy needs," so we began preparing passports, immunizations, and an itinerary by faith.

In Brother Cortez's final service with us, a young man who had recently been paroled from prison stood up and said, "Brother Coker, I don't want to leave this church tonight until I receive the Baptism in the Holy Spirit." As he came forward, Brother Cortez recognized him as the man he and Chet were praying for in his vision. As our people gathered around in a circle while he and Chet prayed for this man, Brother Cortez saw the exact fulfillment of what he had seen in his vision.

Shortly thereafter my father died and a check for fifteen hundred dollars from his estate helped finance our missionary venture. Two weeks before we were to leave, a flood of small contributions began to come in, and by the day we left, we had enough to make the trip. God had fulfilled that part of the prophecy and had supplied our needs.

The three-month missionary journey of Reverend Chester Coker and his family to the Philippines and Korea was carried out on schedule with God graciously fulfilling the promises He made through the prophetic utterance given by Karen Coker and translated by Reverend Cortez. Mrs. Coker's own testimony following their return home documents God's faithfulness.

While we were caught up in the day-to-day ministry in the Philippines and Korea, we didn't have too much time to think about what was happening. But when we returned home and digested the events of the summer, it was staggering. Every promise in the prophecy had been literally fulfilled.

"Many will come before thee receiving the Lord thy God" — From the very first meeting, the response to the gospel was overwhelming. During the crusades in the Philippines we saw over 2,800 persons profess Christ as their Savior, and in South Korea over 600 accepted Christ. Many nights we were unable to sleep after our meeting because of the lasting image of those hungry and seeking faces.

"Filled with the living water" — Wherever we ministered on the Baptism in the Holy Spirit, the altar would be filled with those seeking and receiving the Holy Spirit. We saw many churches strengthened and established as they experienced real revival. Many backsliders were reclaimed and Christians who had allowed divisions to separate them were reconciled to each other.

"Many will be healed in the name of thy God" — Only God knows the number of those who were healed during our meetings. We would offer prayer for the sick and then would move on to new places. We heard many testify to instant healing, and we can say that God did perform miracles before our eyes as we saw God lengthen and straighten arms and legs.

"And thy God will be with thee and supply all thy needs" — Our needs during this time of ministry extended into every realm of life. He kept us mentally and spiritually refreshed when our minds would grow weary from the pressing schedule. We had to rely upon God for our physical needs, as the devil tried to attack us with sickness. In spite of the constant struggle, we managed during the three months to conduct over two hundred meetings, and God was faithful to his promise to supply our financial needs. When we would encounter unexpected expenses, invariably the amount of money we needed would be given or would arrive in the mail.

"And use thee as a great vessel of blessing" — We can only trust that we have been faithful to God and accomplished what He intended that we accomplish. The faith of the dedicated workers of the Philippine Native Crusade, along with its directors, Reverend and Mrs. C. R. Cortez, has been an inspiration and a blessing to us. Nine new congregations were started as a result of our meetings in the Philippines last summer. Theirs is the task of following up on that which God has begun.

Chapter 28

He Didn't *Look* Mexican

March 10, 1972

Dear Mr. Basham,

In the February issue of *New Wine* there was an item stating a request for testimonies to the experience of speaking in tongues in a known language. I would like to share our interesting experience with you.

Last March, at the Charismatic Conference in Tulsa, Oklahoma, Bob Mumford, Derek Prince, and Charles Simpson were ministering, and my husband and I were attending the sessions. The Friday night session was starting and during the time of prayer everyone was worshiping and praising God in English and in tongues. At my left was a young boy really having at it — praising God in such beautiful adoration, in Spanish.

I was praying, too, but couldn't help wondering to myself if the boy was speaking in tongues or if he was speaking his native language. He didn't *look* Mexican, or Puerto Rican, or anything except plain American (whatever that is!).

After the service was over and we were getting ready to leave, I asked the boy if Spanish was his native language or if he had studied it in school. He said no. Then I told him that during the prayer time he had been praying so beautifully in Spanish that it was thrilling to overhear.

His face broke into the most radiant smile, and he reached up and gave me a big hug and said, "Oh, thank you! Thank you! I didn't know what I was saying but I pray in tongues a lot. I don't know how to speak Spanish! I'm only in the ninth grade! I have never studied it in school." He was so thrilled!

I don't know any other language except Spanish. We lived in Spain three years while in the air force, and visited three or four times weekly with dear Spanish friends who don't speak any English. My husband had to use Spanish in his work all the time and has almost a major in Spanish in his university studies. I read the New Testament in Spanish to try to keep up with the language now that we don't have to use it daily.

It was so natural hearing the boy speaking Spanish and if we'd realized at the time that he was speaking in tongues, perhaps we would have tried to listen more attentively. My husband heard the boy speaking Spanish, too, but didn't think anything special of it at the time.

Both my husband and I have been baptized in the Holy Spirit, and I know we would be thrilled, as the boy was, if someone were to hear and identify our prayer language. In the meantime we'll go on enjoying speaking in tongues anyhow.

Yours in Christ,
Dorothy McClendon
Greenville, Texas

Chapter 29

The Miracle of Tongues Among the Roman Catholics

The June 8, 1973, edition of the *Ft. Lauderdale Sun-Sentinental* contained an Associated Press article entitled, "Spirit Movement Praised." It said in part:

"One of Roman Catholicism's most influential prelates has strongly endorsed an American-born free-wheeling Pentecostal Spirit movement rising among the world's Christians.

"Belgium's Leo Joseph Cardinal Suenens said, 'I see it progressing powerfully, growing very fast everywhere . . . . It's no longer just an American phenomenon, but in all countries. It's a world-wide phenomenon.'

"His comments came in a news conference at a gathering of about 22,000 Catholic leaders in the charismatic renewal.

"Besides stress on spontaneous prayer and Bible study, the movement is characterized by gifts of the Spirit such as healing and speaking in unknown tongues to praise God.

" 'It's a new taste of the gospel in its reality and simplicity,' he said. 'It's important that we keep the doors open to this spontaneity. It's an answer to the people's desire to practice faith spontaneously, to express it as they feel it.'

"Cardinal Suenens added, 'It's bringing all Christians together in a very, very close way.' He said he recently discussed the movement with Pope Paul VI who listened openly but did not express an opinion.

"An estimated 300,000 Catholics are now involved in this country, along with growing thousands in main-line Protestant denominations.

"The movement started in 1966 among Roman Catholic college students, after its outbreak in several main-line Protestant denominations. It has since mushroomed among both old and young, many of them now participating in more than 1,250 weekly prayer meetings."

The rise of the charismatic movement within the staid walls of the Roman Catholic Church has been one of the great spiritual surprises of our time. I was privileged to have been present at a house prayer meeting in Pittsburgh, in 1966 when two young Roman Catholic instructors from Duquesne University received the Baptism in the Holy Spirit. Days later, revival broke out on the Duquesne campus, quickly spreading to Notre Dame, then to other Roman Catholic universities, and quickly to many countries around the world.

The primary literary voice for the Catholic charismatic movement is a monthly magazine *New Covenant* published in Ann Arbor, Michigan, with subscribers in eighty-seven countries. In the January 1973 issue, *New Covenant* printed an article entitled, "Identified Tongues," from which we quote.

"One of the most fascinating aspects of the charismatic renewal for many people has been the gift of tongues: for some a steppingstone to a greater yielding to the Lord, for others a stumbling block. On those occasions where a tongue has been identified, though the person speaking it did not know the language, it has always been a testimony to the power of God. Several months ago *New Covenant* asked its readers to share the specifics of times and places when someone spoke in an identified tongue. The response has shown that this is not an isolated, sometime phenomenon. God does use this means to build up His people. We would like to pass on some of what we have received for the same purpose; we have the specifics of time and place available for anyone interested.

"The many testimonies to identified tongues that we have received span the world. They have been living languages as well as languages no people has spoken for centuries. Sometimes the whole message in tongues was in a specific language; sometimes there was a sentence or two in the midst of a message, as though for the one or two people there who would be able to recognize it. The Spirit of God is not limited in His power to time, place, or culture; His work is to draw the entire world under the Lordship of Jesus.

"Europe has figured prominently (perhaps because European languages are more often recognizable by our readers). French, Norwegian, Greek, and others, including Gaelic in two cases, have been identified, though it was certain that the person speaking had no solid knowledge of the language.

"The Far East has been also represented. On several occasions a tongue has been identified and translated as Chinese . . . .

"Africa was also represented. Many have already heard of the instance of Yoruba (a language of Nigeria) being identified in Cochabamba, Bolivia, by an Irish priest (*see* November, 1971, *New Covenant* page 6, for details) . . . .

"The Middle East was the place where tongues were first given and recognized (Acts 2). The number of instances we have received of recognized Middle Eastern tongues was not surprising. In one Michigan prayer meeting, a young woman gave a message in tongues and a Pentecostal minister gave the interpretation. One of the listeners could testify that it was nearly a word-for-word translation of the message, which was in the Greek-Aramaic dialect spoken in Palestine in the first century. Several instances of classical Hebrew excerpts from the psalms praising the Lord for his goodness, or calling his people to trust in Him were recognized as such, and the interpretations verified by persons present who had a good knowledge of Hebrew. One man, on a tour with a mixed group of Jewish and Christian tourists through the Roman catacombs, felt a strong urge to go up to the Hebrew professor who was acting as tour guide and speak to him in tongues. The professor was somewhat surprised, but was easily able to translate from the Aramaic-Hebrew dialect of the third century ("neither before nor after") a sentence in praise of the Lord.

"These instances of recognized tongues speak to us of the mission of the Spirit over the whole earth."

New Covenant editor Ralph Martin, on learning of my work on this book, graciously provided from the files of *New Covenant,* the letters of testimony which comprise the remainder of this chapter.

March 9, 1973
New Covenant Magazine
The Editor
Ann Arbor, Michigan
Dear Sir:

In January of this year, Father Patrick Fernando from Ceylon came to spend some of his vacation with us.

On February 7, 1973, during Bible Study Class, we encouraged Father Patrick to say something in his native language and he did. We had a conversation about the different tongues spoken in Ceylon. Since the language Father had spoken sounded so much like the unknown tongue the Holy Spirit has given me, I asked him to say something in another dialect. Father had only begun speaking when I recognized the phrases and certain sounds as being my unknown tongue. Several of those present suggested that I speak my tongue to the Father to see if he could understand what was being said. Father did confirm that I was speaking in Tamil, a language native to certain parts of Ceylon and India.

There was much joy, especially between Father Patrick and myself, and we shared this good news with our prayer community the next evening. Later, in private conversation with Father, he again confirmed the fact that I was speaking Tamil, and that he understood a great deal of what was said.

At least six members of our community feel that this information should be shared with you and it has been suggested that Father Patrick authenticate this statement. I am asking Father Patrick to co-sign this letter with me. If you require further authentication, let me know, as there were six people present at the Bible study.

To the very best of my knowledge, God has granted me the great favor to speak Tamil words in rendering Him praise. To Him be glory forever and ever.

Joan Deutsch
Odessa, Texas
Father Patrick Fernando

Report by Sister Teresa Doyle, OSF, Savannah, Missouri, January 17, 1973.

Charismatic prayer meetings and programs are often held for nondenominational audiences at a Youth Center in Kansas City, Kansas.

In the spring of 1971, Sister M. Melita, O.S.F. who teaches at St. Therese School, Parkville, Missouri, attended one of these charismatic programs with Mrs. John Fowler. A Catholic priest was one of the speakers of the evening.

After the program, an invitation was given for any who wished to be prayed for to receive the Baptism of the Spirit to come to the prayer room near the auditorium. Sister Melita decided to be prayed for. Mrs. Fowler went with her and joined in with the priest and others who were praying. After a short time of prayer, Sister Melita heard Mrs. Fowler recite the whole "Benedicte" in Latin as we used to recite it in our Latin office before we got the English office.

When Sister Melita remarked afterward how beautifully she said the Latin "Benedicte," Mrs. Fowler told her that she did not know she was praying in Latin, and had never had any Latin experience whatever; that she just prayed in the Spirit.

Both Sister Melita and Mrs. Fowler have given permission for me to tell you of this incident, for which we thank and praise the Lord!

February 10, 1973
Dear Brother In Christ,

Praise the Lord Jesus! My name is Robert Buss and I am a member of the prayer community of "Ezekial 37." We meet at Mt. Saint Peter Roman Catholic Church of New Kensington, Pennsylvania. I have been told you are asking for testimony of people who have had their "tongues" recognized. I would like to offer mine.

About six months ago, after I was praying for some people following the prayer meeting, a young woman asked me if I knew what I was saying when I prayed in tongues. I told her I didn't. She went on to say that her father is Hindustani and that she recognized that what I was saying was in her father's language. It is called Urdo. She repeated some of the words I had said and remarked that they were all words of praise.

Her name is Yvonne Lowe. She is a native of India, has been in this country for three years, and speaks five languages. She is a Montessori teacher at Natrona Heights, Pennsylvania. It was her first time at a prayer meeting.

May the Lord continue to bless your work.

Your brother,
Robert Buss

New Covenant Magazine
The Editor
Ann Arbor, Michigan

Dear Sir:

At the request of Sister Charlotte Schaub, Saint Joseph's Convent, Weir, Michigan, who had been trying to get a prayer group started at Saint Simon's Catholic Church, Ludington, Michigan, a group of eighteen or so members of the Grand Haven Prayer Community travelled to Ludington to hold a prayer meeting with some people from Saint Simon's on June 24, 1971.

Toward the end of the meeting, I was led to speak aloud in

tongues. A Pentecostal minister from Ludington gave the interpretation. After the prayer meeting, Bert Ghezzi asked if anyone had any questions. Father Albesteffer, assistant at Saint Simon's asked me, "How many years of church language have you had?"

I told him, "None, I know only enough Latin to sing in the church choir."

He then asked the Pentecostal minister the same question. He answered, "I have never studied a foreign language of any kind."

Father then said to me, "You spoke flawless Greek-Aramaic dialect, the language believed to have been spoken by Christ." To the minister he said, "And you gave an almost word-for-word translation of what she said."

Sister Charlotte, although she wasn't there that night, could probably give you the name of the Pentecostal minister, and also the names of some of the people from Ludington who remember the incident. Monsignor Bukowski was also there.

Yours in Jesus Christ
Joan McCarthy
Grand Haven, Michigan

The above report from Joan McCarthy prompted a letter from a member of the *New Covenant* staff, asking for more details. Joan McCarthy responded with the following brief letter.

Dear Frank,

Praise the Lord! Sorry that this has taken so long. I saw Sister Charlotte at Grand Valley yesterday for Michigan rededication day. She had seen Rev. Dick Lamphear, Assembly of God Church, Ludington, Michigan. He remembers well the incident I wrote you about and is most willing to have *New Covenant* use his name.

As to the substance of the message: Our Lord said that He loves His people and that He wants them to come to Him united, without discord and division, and to be united to Him and one another in love. Whether they went for the Curcillo (as some wanted) or the charismatic prayer meeting, as others wanted, they should not divide themselves but go one way or the other as a body.

Love in Jesus,
Joan McCarthy

Dear Sirs:

During March, 1972, I became involved in a new prayer group just beginning at Our Lady of Perpetual Help Church in Kenner, Louisiana. At our prayer meetings we have the benediction of the Blessed Sacrament but no Mass.

At our third prayer meeting I spoke out in tongues. Father Benny Pivon asked me later if I had ever studied or could speak Greek: I answered that I could not. He is from Italy and has studied and speaks Greek, and had translated my tongue as saying, "Savior, Savior, Immortal One, have mercy on us."

Love in Christ,
Roy F. Liles, Sr.
New Orleans, La.

Dear Sirs:

While spending the summer in one of the households of the Word of God [the Roman Catholic Charismatic Community in Ann Arbor, Michigan from which the *New Covenant* Magazine issues], I often heard one of my brothers begin his prayer in tongues with the same words. I could not identify the language but I knew just how he said the words, where the accents fell, etc. In fact, I secretly thought it a little monotonous. My summer studies concentrate on the literature of modern Africa but I am also doing some background reading in the older traditional African literature. One evening, as I read an article on the technique of public recitation which included examples transcribed with rhythmic markings, I was startled to see the exact phrase with which this young man, who is an American of Swedish descent and who has had no contact with South Africa, was beginning his prayer: *U sishay' akasishayek (i)*.

The line is the opening of an epic poem of praise of Shaka, a great Zulu king and unifier of his nation in the early nineteenth century. I sat there, checking my memory of what I had so often heard, partly hoping there would be a significant discrepancy because the Zulus had not been acquainted with Christianity at that time and I was wary of what the line might mean. It being identical, accents and all, I looked up the translation: "He who can strike a blow, but whom no man can attack" (Melodic Features in Zulu Eulogistic Recitation by David Rycroft, *African Language Studies* I, 1960).

I praised God, for I realized how apt a description this is. If we desire a truly mutual relationship with God, it must be based on love. He has already allowed his beloved son to suffer the full force of our wrath and to bear the full weight of our sins. Christ, having risen from the dead, dies now no longer. He is beyond our reach as long as we are his enemies, but he is also our judge, one "who can strike a blow, but whom no man can attack." He comes in contact with us directly only when we repent and turn to him in faith. He then makes us his friends, shares his life with us, unites us with Himself in the bond of love.

Phil O'Mara

Dear Sirs:

Re: Tongues and Interpretation.

A few weeks ago, at our Sunday prayer meeting, a woman spoke out in tongues. At that meeting, for the first time, was a religious Sister from the Philippines. Speaking to me later she said, "I don't know what language the first part was, but in the middle of the message I heard a sentence in my language which meant, 'Build up the church!' I listened to hear if that would come in the interpretation — and it did — right in the middle of it! It was so beautiful!"

Sister Gyneth Roberts

Ottawa , Ontario, Canada

Epilogue

In these pages we have shared over thirty personal testimonies to the miracle of tongues — true stories of God's supernatural power at work in the lives of His children. Because of our continuing interest in recording such events, we invite all who have had an experience similar to those in this book to share it with us. The additional testimonies we will use either to expand a later edition of this book or to produce a second volume. After all, our troubled world needs all the good news it can find.

Now, having shared the testimony of many others, perhaps it is permissible to conclude with a more personal word. From the time the idea of this book first came several years ago, I began asking God to verify, for me personally, the reality I wanted to write about. In His own time, and in two different ways, God did exactly that. On one occasion I was a participant, on the other a grateful witness.

The first incident took place in 1969. I was the speaker at the Cleveland, Ohio, chapter meeting of the Full Gospel Business Men's Fellowship International. During the meeting, I had shared personal testimony combined with some instruction for those desiring to receive the Baptism in the Holy Spirit with speaking in tongues.

At the close of the meeting, some sixty-five or seventy persons remained for prayer. As we prayed, many received and began to praise God in new languages. As was my custom, I moved around the prayer room encouraging various ones by speaking softly but aloud, switching intermittently from praying in tongues to giving instructions and encouragement in English, than back to praying in tongues.

Out of the corner of my eye, I noticed a young man following me around. I assumed he was one of the younger officers of the chapter who wanted to be helpful. When the time of ministry was concluded, he came over to me with some excitement.

"Reverend Basham, I hope my following you around didn't upset you," he began.

"No," I assured him, "but I did wonder why you were doing it."

"Well," he explained, "the first time I heard you praying in tongues with someone, I thought I understood some of the words you were speaking. So I followed you to make sure, and I did! Five times I heard you, as you prayed in tongues encouraging others. You were speaking Spanish and you were saying over and over, 'I will praise Him, I will praise Him.' "

At his words, a kind of quiet elation spread through me. "Thank you, Lord," I said to myself. "At last, it has happened to me!"

The second incident occurred a year later, in a meeting only seventy miles from the first. Again I was the speaker in a Full Gospel Business Men's Fellowship International chapter meeting, this time in Youngstown, Ohio.

At the close of my testimony, someone spoke a message in tongues. After a moment of silence, a Pentecostal minister I knew brought the interpretation. It was a deeply reassuring message of God's love, and was highly edifying to the meeting.

Then something else happened, which at first puzzled me. A second man stood and gave a message in tongues in a strange staccato-sounding language, unlike any I had heard before. Again the room grew silent as we waited for the interpretation, but there was none. As the silence lengthened, I silently asked God if I should attempt the interpretation. Sometimes I receive the interpretation to tongues, but this time nothing came. I glanced at some of the other chapter officers to see if any of them were prompted to bring the interpretation, and they merely shrugged.

So I closed the meeting with prayer, concluding that the man who had spoken the second message had been impulsive and had spoken out loud when he should have prayed to himself. After all, the Scriptures say that if there is no interpreter, the one speaking in tongues should "keep silence . . . and speak to himself and to God" (I Corinthians 14:28).

But I soon discovered that God had His purpose in allowing the uninterpreted tongue. After the benediction, one of the chapter officers introduced me to a young serviceman recently returned from Vietnam. The young man could speak Vietnamese, having served with an intelligence unit assigned to interrogate prisoners. Although a Christian, he held strong dispensationalist convictions, believing the age of miracles was past and that the charismatic movement was spurious.

"I came tonight just to please a friend," the young GI admitted.

He remained critical through the entire evening, unimpressed with the singing, the testimonies, and the message. He also totally rejected the first message in tongues followed by interpretation as a "put-up job."

It was the second message in tongues which shook him to

the core, for while the man who spoke knew no language but English and had never traveled outside the United States, nevertheless he prayed a beautiful prayer in *flawless Vietnamese*. The young serviceman had heard and understood every word!

Paul clearly indicates that speaking in tongues can be a "sign to them that believe not" (I Corinthians 14:22). The young man left the meeting that night with a drastically altered theology, and I left grateful to God for having witnessed personally the effect of the miracle of tongues on an unbeliever.

I have come to the conclusion that nothing quite compares with personal testimony to such experiences. In the final analysis, testimony has an effect on the skeptic and the unbeliever which no amount of teaching or preaching can provide. John, chapter 9, records the story of Jesus healing a man who had been blind from birth. The man's testimony created a great stir in the town. Theological controversy flared all around him. The religious authorities even tried intimidating his parents, but no one could deny the miracle and his testimony could not be shaken. "One thing I know, that whereas I was blind, now I see!" (John 9:25)

Personal confidence in God's miracle-working power is one of the most oft-recurring notes sounded through these pages. The miracle of tongues can create faith, can strengthen faith, or can restore faith which has been lost. Chapter fourteen told how a dying man accepted Christ as his Saviour because he witnessed the miracle of tongues. Other chapters reveal how God spoke prophetic words of comfort and gave promise of restoration to those who had fallen away from Him.

Another quality we find woven like a golden thread through these pages is that of unmitigated joy. Admittedly, joy has not been a dominant characteristic of the church in our day, yet it is one of the fruits of the Spirit (Galatians 5:22) meant to enhance our witness to Christ's love for us. As these pages have abundantly testified, God's intervention in our lives in a miraculous way may accomplish in an instant what other religious activity has failed to produce in years.

"My feet haven't touched the ground since . . . ."

"My grateful heart overflowed . . . ."

"It is not difficult to imagine the overflowing joy in both of us as we realized the miracle . . . ."

Perhaps we have forgotten how God delights in giving His children lovely spiritual surprises, and the surprise miracle of tongues often proves to be the springboard to lasting spiritual joy.

Finally, there is one more truth revealed in these pages, which I believe to be the most significant of all; namely, that Christianity is a miracle-working religion. I don't believe God ever intended it to be anything less. From the beginning, miraculous signs and wonders were to accompany the preaching of the gospel (Mark 16:15–20). The clear teaching of Scripture shows us how God's miracle-working power is given as an encouragement to all who love and trust Him, and these testimonies prove that His power is as available to us as it was to those rugged and daring disciples who first fell in love with Jesus.

Thank God He has not changed! "Jesus Christ the same, yesterday, today and forever" (Hebrews 13:8).

If these testimonies have served to create faith in the unbeliever, to strengthen faith in the faltering believer, or to restore faith to the fallen believer, then this book has accomplished its purpose.